967 w57

Jay P. Maggart

THE ART OF WHISTLER

THE
ART OF WHISTLER

BY

ELIZABETH ROBINS PENNELL

WITH

JOSEPH PENNELL,

AUTHOR OF "LIFE OF WHISTLER" AND
THE "WHISTLER JOURNAL"

WITH THIRTY-TWO REPRODUCTIONS
IN THE AQUATONE PROCESS

THE MODERN LIBRARY
PUBLISHERS : NEW YORK

CONTENTS

ILLUSTRATIONS

PAINTINGS

vii

INTRODUCTION

JOSEPH PENNELL and I were to have written this book together. We had planned it, but when Death claimed him the work had gone scarcely further than the plan. He did not live to fill it with the life and energy he gave to everything he did, with the vigorous eloquence that came of his love for the truth and his strong convictions. However, I know what his ideas for the book were and, also, as his collaborator in *The Life of Whistler*, I share his unfailing sense of responsibility in all that concerns the great artist he honored as master and who honored us by appointing us his biographers. He wished to show Whistler as he was, not as his contemporaries imagined him to be, not as posterity might believe him to have been had he survived solely in the legends that grew up about his personality and his art. From the time we undertook the biography we spared no trouble to obtain the facts and expose the legends. Joseph Pennell's interest never weakened and I hope mine may not now I am left to finish my task unaided.

It is little less than a quarter of a century since Whistler died. Fashions among artists have come and gone with incredible rapidity in that short period. Numerous "Isms" have been developed, have flourished, and have perished. To the exponents of the new creeds Whistler seemed a back number, and they endeavored to destroy his reputation by faint praise, dismissing him as insignificant both in his achievement and his influence. At the best, they declared, his sphere was limited. His painting had charm perhaps, but it was of the slightest. His etching was mere reporting. He worked only in two dimensions. And nowhere on canvas or paper, on stone or copper, did he reveal that struggle for self-expression which, to be in the mode, one must now esteem as greater than actual accomplishment. But the Prophets of "Modernism" have already had their day and others arise in their place to herald the next phase in the progress of art.

Art, however, has nothing to do with fashion, nothing with progress. It happens as Whistler said, and in its happening is perfect. Already the pendulum of popular opinion, that was threatening to swing far from Whistler, is swinging rapidly back to him. Nor is this surprising. The popular gods of the critics rise and fall with the passing generations. In my young days, when Whistler hailed "The Master of Madrid," when R. A. M. Stevenson wrote his memorable book about Velasquez, there was dismay among the Ruskinites. To-day I hear that Rubens is fast supplanting Velasquez in certain critical camps, while one critic, a German, has suddenly discovered El Greco—whom artists have long known and appreciated—and to accept a new master is for this Columbus to knock down the old. Velasquez is relegated to his proper rank as a photographer in paint, or as first bored celebrant of boredom, if you accept Yeats as an authority. But, with the next turn of the wheel, Rubens and El Greco will be the fallen idols. The more criticism changes, the more it is the same, and as it was yesterday, as it is to-day, so it will be to-morrow. The critics will continue to imagine vain things and make strange discoveries, but the great artists of all time will survive praise and blame alike, and among these great artists Whistler will hold a high place.

This place was accorded to him grudgingly during his lifetime, that is, by the many. The few, of course, understood. The many could not offer as excuse for their blindness Whistler's habit of keeping himself out of their sight, for he always kept himself in it. He never shared the fancy of his contemporary Matthys Maris for strict seclusion in the forgotten room of some mean London street. He preferred to fight his battles in public, to challenge "the enemies" to open combat. He needed no dealer to force him to exhibit. His was the "joyous" task of bidding the unbelievers come and look at the work that bewildered and shocked them. In the quarter of the century since his death little has been added, except in details, to the knowledge of the man and the artist for those who already knew and understood. No unknown masterpiece has come to light, though fakes have not been spared us. Unpublished and hitherto unquoted letters have figured in the sale rooms but they have only confirmed his reputation as a wit and a warrior in the defense of art, have only shown him again in the splendid gayety of his intervals of leisure, the unfailing seriousness of his hours of work. His profession of faith as artist was made before his death in *The Gentle Art,* his "Bible" and, of the innumerable books on art, one of the exceptions that live and will live. He did not leave it to posterity to explain him and interpret his art. He explained himself, he was his art's own interpreter. He was proof against the laughter that greeted explanation and interpretation both. With his clear vision he foresaw the day when the public that ridiculed him would itself be held up to ridicule.

And he was right. If the knowledge of the man and the artist has been increased and strengthened only in details, the years have made this all-important difference. The ridicule is a thing of the past. He is no longer the charlatan of a day, but one of "the saving remnant" in art who remain, whose influence must be reckoned with. He towers above his contemporaries, he cannot be altogether ignored by those historians of art who are least in sympathy with him, his end has not been the rubbish heap of forgotten reputations and exploded genius. The critics who treated him as a butt for laughter and mirth would not be as much as remembered had he not set them on a high pillory for the derision of the ages. Even Ruskin has ceased to exist as critic, surviving as the master of words, "whose writing is art," to whom Whistler—the "coxcomb"—had the nobility to pay this tribute. Whistler's fellow artists who would have none of him, who jeered with the jeering crowd, have disappeared, are almost unheard of. Who thinks now of Tadema, Leighton, Poynter, Richmond, of any of the Academic heroes of his day? It is the Idle Apprentice whose memory endures, the bankrupt chased from the modest White House close to the river he loved, while they flourished in their St. John's Wood and Kensington palaces. The present Bolshevism of the studios cannot destroy him. He will outlive the Bolshevists whose power is undermined by their own defiance of tradition. Whistler believed in himself, yes. But still stronger was his belief in art, its history already complete in the accomplishment of the past, though the chosen "with the mark of the Gods upon him" may never again appear. He was thought a rebel, a Bolshevist, before the name was invented. But his rebellion was against the commonplaces, the conventions, the hypocrisies of the studios, against the use, the abuse of art as a moral or a social or an educational prop for the mistaken missionary. Art meant nothing more nor less to him than the "Science of Beauty," and he held that it is for each artist, as generation succeeds generation, to equip himself technically, the humble student of this Beauty, and carry on the tradition of the great past.

ELIZABETH ROBINS PENNELL

NEW YORK CITY—1927

BIOGRAPHICAL TABLE OF DATES

1834   July 10th. Whistler born at Lowell, Massachusetts.

1837   The Whistler family moved to Stonington, Connecticut.

1840   Major Whistler appointed Chief Engineer of the Western Railroad and the family moved to Springfield, Massachusetts.

1842   Major Whistler, invited by Nicholas I to build the railroad from St. Petersburg to Moscow, started for Russia.

1843   Whistler, with his mother and brothers, joined Major Whistler in St. Petersburg.

1845   Whistler began his study of Art in the Imperial Academy of Fine Arts.

1849   Major Whistler died on April 9th and Whistler returned with his family to Stonington, moved to Pomfret and was sent to the Rev. Dr. Roswell Park's School.

1851   July 1st. Whistler entered the United States Military Academy, West Point, Colonel Robert E. Lee the Commandant.

1854   June 16th. Whistler discharged from the U. S. Army for deficiency in chemistry.

1854   November 7th. Whistler appointed to the Drawing Division of the United States Coast and Geodetic Survey.

1855   Whistler resigned from the U. S. Coast and Geodetic Survey and went to Paris to study art.

1859   *At the Piano,* turned down at the *Salon,* was, with the other rejected pictures of the year, shown in Bonvin's studio where Whistler first met Courbet. *The French set: Twelve Etchings from Nature* published in London.

1860   Whistler began to make London his headquarters, and exhibited for the first time in the Royal Academy; *At the Piano* and five etchings hung.

1862   *The White Girl* rejected at the Royal Academy, shown in the Berners Street Gallery, its criticism bringing from Whistler the first of his letters to the press.

1863   Whistler established in a house of his own, No. 7 Lindsey Row, now 101 Cheyne Walk, Chelsea.

1864   The famous *Hommage à Delacroix* by Fantin Latour, Whistler prominent in the group, exhibited at the *Salon.*

1865   *The Little White Girl* in the Royal Academy, verses from Swinburne's *Before the Mirror,* inspired by it, printed on the gold paper of the frame.

1866   The year of Whistler's unaccountable journey to Valparaiso. On his return he moved into No. 2 Lindsey Row.

1867   His first exhibition (at the French Gallery) of a Nocturne, one of the two Valparaiso Harbors: *Crépuscule in Flesh Color and Green.* Represented in the Universal Exposition in Paris. His *Two Little White Girls* in the Royal Academy, damned by P. G. Hamerton, the abuse a challenge for the "joyous" answer preserved in *The Gentle Art*.

1871   The *Thames Set* of etchings—*Sixteen Etchings of Scenes on the Thames*—published by Ellis and Green.

1872   Whistler's portrait of his Mother exhibited in the Royal Academy, the last painting by him ever hung on its walls.

1874   Whistler opened his first "one-man" Exhibition at No. 48 Pall Mall, including in it the great full length portraits of the period and some of the Nocturnes. Percy Thomas issued the first Catalogue of Whistler's etchings.

1876   Whistler began the decoration of *The Peacock Room*.

1877   Whistler finished the decoration of *The Peacock Room*, quarreled with Leyland, the quarrel the cause eventually of his bankruptcy. The year of the first Grosvenor Gallery Exhibition, Whistler showing among other things *The Falling Rocket*, the cause of Ruskin's attack in *Fors Clavigera*. Whistler sued Ruskin for libel.

1878   In October, Whistler moved into the White House. In November the Whistler-Ruskin case was tried in the Exchequer Division at Westminster. In December Chatto & Windus published *Whistler* v. *Ruskin—Art and Art Critics*, the first of his pamphlets in brown paper covers.

1879   In May, Whistler declared bankrupt, the White House sold, and Whistler started for Venice.

1880   In November, Whistler returned from Venice to London, held an exhibition of his Venice etchings at the Fine Art Society's, the first of his much talked about Bond Street "one-man" Exhibitions, the Catalogue of each issued in brown paper covers.

1881   Mrs. Whistler, his mother, died at Hastings. Whistler took a studio at No. 13 Tite Street. The year of the Duveneck misunderstanding in the Painter-Etchers' Society, and the publication of Whistler's *Piker Papers.*—The portrait of his Mother exhibited at The Pennsylvania Academy of the Fine Arts, and Philadelphia lost the chance of acquiring it at the price of a thousand dollars, as New York did the following year.

1883   The "Mother" in the *Salon*. Whistler awarded a third-class medal, the only award he ever received at the *Salon*.

1884   Joseph Pennell first met Whistler. Whistler elected to membership in the Society of British Artists.

1885   February 20th. Whistler gave his *Ten O'Clock* at Prince's Hall, London, repeating it the same year before the British Artists and at Cambridge and Oxford. Moved his studio to 454 Fulham Road. Lived first in a small house, he called "The Pink Palace," close by, and then in The Vale, Chelsea.

1886   June 1st. Whistler elected President of the Society of British Artists.

1887   The year of Queen Victoria's Jubilee. Whistler prepared an illuminated address from the Society which, in return, was allowed by the Queen to call itself "Royal."

1888   June 4th, Whistler resigned from the Royal Society of British artists. Chatto & Windus published *Ten O'Clock* in a brown paper covered pamphlet. Moved to the Tower House, Chelsea. On August 11th, married Beatrix Godwin, widow of E. W. Godwin. Second Class medal from the International Exhibition at Munich, acknowledged as "second-hand compliment."

1889   Whistler made Chevalier of the Legion of Honor and Honorary Member of the Bavarian Royal Academy, eventually receiving Gold Medal and Cross of St. Michael. Gold medals awarded him at the Paris Universal Exposition and at Amsterdam. To celebrate these honors a public dinner given him at the Criterion, London. Official recognition his at last.

1890   Whistler moved back to Cheyne Walk, No. 21.— William Heinemann published *The Gentle Art of Making Enemies*.

1891   The Glasgow Corporation purchased the *Carlyle*. The *Mother* bought by the French Government for the Luxembourg.

1892   The definite Turn of the Tide. Whistler's Exhibition of *Nocturnes*, *Marines*, and *Chevalet Pieces* at the Goupil Gallery in London—his "heroic kick in Bond-Street." Having gone back to Paris to live, took an apartment in the Rue du Bac, No. 110, and a studio at No. 86 Rue Notre Dame-des-Champs.

1894   The beginning of Mrs. Whistler's long illness.—Gold Medal awarded by the Academy in Philadelphia.

1895   The Eden Trial before the Civil Tribunal in Paris—judgment against Whistler.—Gold Medal from Antwerp.—A year of wandering between France and England in search of health for Mrs. Whistler.

1896   Mrs. Whistler died at Hampstead on May 10th, buried at Chiswick on the 14th.

1897   Whistler a witness for Joseph Pennell in the Lithograph case brought against *The Saturday Review*.

1897   Whistler took the Eden Case to the Cour de Cassation. Trial on November 17th. Judgment in the higher Court in Whistler's favor. The first meeting of the International Society held in December in London.

1898   Whistler elected first Chairman, then first President of the International Society. The first exhibition opened in May. Madame Carmen Rossi established the Académie Carmen in the Passage Stanislas, Paris, Whistler promising to visit the classes and criticize the students' work.

1899   Henry May published in Paris *The Baronet and the Butterfly*.

1900   Whistler asked Joseph and E. R. Pennell to write

his Life. Received a *Grand Prix* for painting and one for engraving at the Paris Universal Exposition. Many journeys for his own health now began. A flurried period between Paris and London, with occasional wanderings to the sea. At the end of the year started for Corsica.

1901   Winter in Corsica. The Académie Carmen closed. Returned in May to London, where the greater part of the last few years had been spent, and now gave up the Rue du Bac apartment and Paris Studio. In the early winter left London for Bath.

1902   The winter in Bath. Much weaker on his return to London in March. Again took a house in Chelsea, No. 74 Cheyne Walk. In June went to Holland with Charles L. Freer. Was seriously ill in The Hague. Recovered sufficiently to return to No. 74 Cheyne Walk at the end of the summer.

1903   An invalid all winter. Received the degree of LL.D. from Glasgow University. Was appointed Chairman of the London Committee of the Art Department of the Universal Exposition to be held at St. Louis in 1904. Whistler died on Friday, July 17th. The funeral service in the old Chelsea Church on Wednesday, July 22d. Buried in the old Chiswick Graveyard where Hogarth lies.

THE ART OF WHISTLER

I

WHISTLER THE MAN: HIS GAYETY

WHISTLER had no private life, he once told a foolish person who threatened to expose it. He was right. He left no chance to the modern inventors of private lives for the great whom Death has delivered into their hands. An extraordinary thing about this extraordinary man was that everything he did, everything he said, became public property. No one else was ever so talked about as he was during his life, as he is to this day. After he asked Joseph Pennell and myself to write his biography, we subscribed to Press Agencies in New York, London and Paris for all newspaper notices of him and his work and there must be some hundred and fifty large volumes filled with these clippings in The Collection of Whistleriana we presented to the Library of Congress. It is unbelievable, and no less unbelievable is the number of magazine articles and books that began to be written about him as soon as he was in his grave and that continue to be written about him now, when almost a quarter of a century has passed. It would seem as if the world could not have enough of him and his affairs.

More extraordinary, and more unbelievable, is the fact that, despite all this writing and talking about him, never has a man been less understood, more misrepresented. I do not for a minute mean to picture him as the Great Misunderstood to be wept over and defended and upheld. No one knew better than he how to take care of himself. He would have despised tears. He was his own best defender. He was keen and eloquent in upholding his principles, fearless in living his life as he wanted to live it. But this is just what puzzled the public, the standardized public that looks upon character, individuality, anything different, as eccentricity. Whistler had enough individuality to stock a regiment. Therefore, to his own generation he was a poseur, a trifler, a jester, a quarrelsome mountebank. He was at no pains to correct this impression. If people choose to be bewildered, well, let him have the joy of catering to the bewilderment. And he did, with the result that the idea of the man as poseur and jester endures, though it has been less easy to deny his greatness as artist.

I knew Whistler well during his later years; as collaborator in writing his life I obtained from others that knowledge of him in his earlier years

which I could not supply myself. With the facts
at my disposal, it is clear to me how the misunderstanding arose. There is none so blind as he who re-
fuses to see and the public has persistently refused
to see not so much that Whistler was gay, a truth
too obvious to escape the least observant eye, but
that his gayety was the very keystone to his character. Whistler was by nature one of the gayest men
who ever lived, just as he was one of the most serious artists, a rare combination, incomprehensible
to the average intelligence. As a man he was gayety
itself. He loved to be gay, to have gay people about
him, to do gay things, to be "joyous"—joyousness
is the motive running all through *The Gentle Art*
—"joyous" and "gay" are the two words repeated,
like a beloved refrain, over and over again in his
talk and his letters with no rival unless it is
"amazing." He needed to laugh, to see life humor-
ously. He was an enemy to long faces. No one
worked harder than he did, but he did not believe
in doing his work as if it were a task. Until he was
embittered by constant misrepresentation, he looked
upon life as a pleasure to be made the most of joy-
fully, not as a penance to be carried out with sighs
and groanings. He was no Jeremiah.

From his childhood up, his gayety struck every
one who knew or met him. It was an incessant
anxiety to his mother, a Puritan after her fashion,
a distributor of tracts abroad and at home a strict

disciplinarian. With the recitation of the Psalms the day's routine for her children began, and the chief end of her training was to keep her boys "in the straight and narrow path," to which "high spirits" did not seem the surest guide. Her Diary is full of the heights these spirits reached in her Jamie during the Russian days when Major Whistler, the father, was building the railroad from St. Petersburg to Moscow. She was sorely troubled when, in public, Jamie's "animation" called attention to him, for "ebullition of joy" was surprising to the grave and decorous St. Petersburg crowds. When she went shopping she preferred to take her Willie who was "rather less excitable than Jemmie and therefore more tractable," the gentlest of her dear boys. She was no less disturbed when in the meantime her excitable Jamie got a good drenching out in the Canal, and when, later, at a dinner given her at Tsarskoé Seló, he and Willie, the "tractable" Willie easily led, drained their glasses of champagne as they stood up of their own accord to drink *Santé à l'Empereur*. She could but note with apprehension how, at a review of troops, he made the officers laugh by his remarks, and at Peterhoff was so "saucy" as to laugh himself at Peter the Great's adventures with a paint box. On her return to the United States, after Major Whistler's death, this excitable spirit in her Jamie continued to distress her for even she mistook for a

PORTRAIT OF WHISTLER IN THE BIG HAT,
Freer Collection

failing the fine gayety with which he faced every stage, every crisis, in his life.

As "full of fun" he was remembered by his schoolmates in the Pomfret School, to which he was now sent, making irresistible caricatures, mimicking the pompous headmaster, turning the caning he got for it into a lark. Nor at West Point could the uniform subdue his natural gayety. As full of fun his fellow cadets also remembered him; as gay in his misdemeanors, whether flirtations with French maids in forbidden places at forbidden hours, or absences, or carelessness in details of dress; gay in his excuses for them—hunting for his cat, though no cadet was allowed to keep animals of any kind, was the excuse for his philandering with the French maid; gay over his mistakes in class and tumbles at cavalry drill; gay in his caricatures of officers and examiners and cadets; gay when dismissed from the Academy for failure in Chemistry:—

"I am required to discuss silicon. Silicon is a gas—"

"That will do, Mr. Whistler," said his examiner.

"And," said Whistler years afterward, "had silicon been a gas I would be a Major-General."

It was rare to find him at a loss for an answer when he had not the right one.

"What!" said another examiner, "you do not know the date of the Battle of Buena Vista? Suppose you were to go out to dinner and the company began to talk of the Mexican War, and you, a West Point man, were asked the date of the battle, what would you do?"

"Do?" answered Whistler, "why, I should refuse to associate with people who could talk of such things at dinner!"

Again, in the United States Coast and Geodetic Survey office, the memories were of his gayety out of office hours rather than of his application in them, of his irresponsible treatment of Government copper plates, so that after not many months every one agreed with him that Government business was no affair of his and that the one place where he belonged by right was Paris.

The Latin Quarter was then still in all its glory, its joyousness as yet undimmed, *La Vie de Bohème* in full swing. Whistler knew Murger by heart and loved the book. It might seem as if where to be gay was the rule, his gayety would pass unnoticed. And yet it became the talk of the Latin Quarter. The British students said that he was so gay he never worked and with them the misinterpretation of his gayety began. They carried to London his reputation as the Idle Apprentice, the youth too indefatigably gay to be anything else. He was gay, let no one question that. He was *le Petit Whistler, le petit blagueur, le petit rageur* even to the French students—his "no-shirt friends," the British described them—who had no objection to be gay themselves. Whatever he found to do, that he did with all his might. He played the Latin Quarter game according to rule and with unsparing zest. He dressed the part, his hat with the low crown and broad brim, straw in summer, felt in winter, set jauntily on the black curls, was conspicuous on the *Rive Gauche* where the less anybody dressed like everybody on the other bank, the more conventional he was. His allowance of three hundred and fifty dollars a year was princely in a community where most men depended on their wits. But that did not keep him long from the *Mont de Piété*, the haunt of the student. He lived up his six flights of stairs, in his garret with the best of them, would eat his washstand one week and his wardrobe the next, as he explained to an American from home who had looked him up and was distressed to find him in such poverty-stricken surroundings. He would pawn his coat in summer and go in shirt-sleeves for a cooling drink, and stay a prisoner all night in the Halles until some one would come along and pay for his supper. He did his duty at the *Bal Bullier* and every other students' ball in the Quarter. He had friends among the grisettes, *Fumette* of the etching, *Tigresse* the *Quartier's* name for her, the little *modiste* who in a rage one day tore up a pile of his drawings and reduced him to tears. And he had friends among the professional dancers, *Finette* who excelled in the *Cancan*, but is surprisingly stately and dignified in the portrait he etched of her. He threw himself into the life of the *Quartier* so thoroughly that for the next generation he was the hero of its every legend. "All stories of larks were put down to Whistler," George Boughton said when he, in his turn, went to Paris as a student.

But, as Lincoln was eager to give Grant's brand of whisky to his other generals, so the less stolid students must have wished they could borrow Whistler's brand of idleness for it was astonishing how much this youth who never worked managed to accomplish. During the years he was establishing his reputation as Idle Apprentice he made the etchings of *The French Set*, among his finest of any period; he painted *La Mère Gérard*, the *Head of an Old Man Smoking*, himself in the famous big hat, and *At the Piano*. This last picture was thrown out at the *Salon* of 1859 but hung in an exhibition of the year's rejected held by Bonvin in his studio. There Courbet—the great man, the great independent, the great revolutionary, of the day—saw it and was impressed. If all students could be idly gay to the same purpose, the world would be over-crowded with masterpieces.

After 1859 Whistler spent less time in Paris than in London where gayety never was, never could be a matter of course, is, rather, highly suspicious, almost a crime. The Briton could make nothing of

AT THE PIANO, *Edmund Davis Collection*

his exuberance, his high spirits, his astonishingly original clothes. His hats disturbed all their preconceived notions of what hats should be, and they were paralyzed the summer day when he appeared carrying two umbrellas, a black in case of rain, a white in hope of sunshine. He was always ready for a dance or a masquerade, he played in private theatricals, he was the central figure of every party, every reception, every dinner to which he was bidden. Artists, oppressed with their own seriousness, asked where was there time for serious work? When he went down the river and stayed in shabby, tumbled-down riverside inns, and was making his Thames etchings and painting his *Thames in Ice* and *Wapping*, there were more dinners and dances and songs, and friends to spread the report of them. Wherever he worked people were always about him. He never wanted to be by himself. For several years his faithful companion was Jo, his first model, the beautiful Irish girl with the red hair and the pale, hauntingly sad face, a sadness that impressed Swinburne.

> *Love, is there sorrow hidden,*
> *Is there delight?*

he asked when he saw her portrait in *The Little White Girl*. Jo lived with Whistler in his Cheyne Walk house until his mother arrived from the

United States and the Civil War to join him in London. Other models came and went. Friends pursued him. Hangers-on imposed upon him, but if they amused him they were welcome. He liked people, best of all those who were amusing. The drolleries of life—drollery, another word often in his mouth—appealed to him, stimulated him. It was the dull man he could not stand. His revolt against dullness was the cause of what too often was mistaken for rudeness. A typical incident, often quoted, is that of the American who came up to him one evening at the Carlton Hotel and, as excuse, said they were both born in Lowell within a year of each other, and Whistler told him: "I shall be born when and where I want, and I do not choose to be born at Lowell and I refuse to be sixty-seven." This was thought shocking bad manners and an absurd denial of his age and his birthplace, when Whistler was simply ridding himself of a bore.

In the early Sixties one of his haunts was Tudor House, a little further down Cheyne Walk, where Meredith and Swinburne lived with Gabriel Rossetti, and where William Michael Rossetti, Sandys, and the amazing Howell were constant visitors. To the end he had an affection for Gabriel Rossetti—"the only white man in all the London crowd of painters," I have heard him say, and *un grand artiste* was his description to Fantin. If his friendship for the man never wavered, his admiration for the artist soon dwindled. Rossetti painted the anecdote in vogue during the Victorian era, though it was of another kind and told in another way from the Academician's. Once Rossetti showed Whistler his picture and read him his sonnet inspired by the same subject. "Why not frame the sonnet?" asked Whistler. But Rossetti's art was no drawback to Whistler's joy in a certain droll extravagance in Rossetti's habits and amusements. He saw humor in the sort of menagerie Rossetti kept in his back garden where his "Bull of Bashan" chased him, where his monkeys escaped to the neighboring roofs and peered down upon him from behind chimneys, where his peacock and gazelle fought on the lawn. Whistler never tired of telling the story of the wombat, brought in after dinner with the cigars to be exhibited, curling up in an empty cigar box, forgotten in the heat of argument, and discovered, a complete skeleton, weeks and weeks afterwards. And Whistler's joy was as irrepressible in the droll company of Rossetti's friends. He could laugh to the last over Meredith's pomposities, his rotund periods, his melodramatic poses. He could delight in Swinburne's effeminate affectations as he sat at the feet of Mrs. Whistler and sulked if she would not call him Algernon. His delight was still greater in Frederick Sandys, always bankrupt, always on the

way to the laundry with his white waistcoat in a
brown paper parcel under his arm, always in quest
of "five hundred, you know," always magnificent.
Whistler saw fun even in William Michael Rossetti, dull, kindly, the most unexpected sort of
brother for Gabriel. He was rather the butt of
some of the more outspoken in the Pre-Raphaelite
circle. There was another evening, when William
Morris was boring them all with the story of one
of his Norse heroes and Gabriel Rossetti could endure it no longer and broke in at last to say he
didn't think much of a hero who had a dragon or
a serpent for a brother. "I'd a great deal rather
have a dragon for a brother than a damned fool,"
roared Morris, and probably no more was heard
that evening of Norse adventurers and their relations. But Whistler's chief favorite was Howell—
Charles Augustus Howell, one of the most picturesque figures of a picturesque period, "the Gil-
Blas-Robinson-Crusoe hero out of his proper
time," "the superb liar" in Whistler's words, immortalized by Rossetti in a famous limerick:

> There's a Portuguee person called Howell,
> Who lays on his lies with a trowel;
>   When I goggle my eyes,
>   And start with surprise,
> 'Tis at the monstrous big lies told by Howell.

THE COAST OF BRITTANY, ALONE WITH THE TIDE, *Wadsworth Atheneum*

At first, during these early London years, Whistler's laughter was never embittered. He played hard because to him life was impossible without play. He worked harder because art was his absorbing interest. The pictures this trifler, this Idle Apprentice, was painting at the time, live to-day, almost all fill a distinguished place in national collections—*The Music Room*, *Alone with the Tide*, *The Blue Wave*, *The Last of Old Westminster*, *The White Girl*. Not even the turning down of *The White Girl* at the Royal Academy in 1862 disturbed, if it disappointed him. Besides, it fared much as *At the Piano* had fared in Paris, its rejection proving, if anything, an asset. An exhibition of the Academy's rejected was held in the Berners Street Gallery where *The White Girl* was hung, catalogued as *The Woman in White*, the title of Wilkie Collins' then widely read novel. The title led a clever critic, who thought the painting a "bizarre production," to point out that the face was well done, but it was not that of Mr. Wilkie Collins' *Woman in White*, and this criticism led to Whistler's first letter to the press. Nothing could sound less like Whistler, not a hint in it of the letters that were later to exasperate "the serious ones of this earth" and to be collected in *The Gentle Art*. It explains simply, quite amiably, "I had no intention whatever of illustrating Mr. Wilkie Collins' novel; it so happens, indeed, that I have never read it." But because the letter is not remarkable, because it is so different from the letters preserved in *The Gentle Art*, it holds an important place in any study of Whistler, characteristic of him as he was before forced to arm himself in self-defense.

He could take hard knocks as well as any man. He knew that his paintings were not "uncouth," "smudgy," "eccentric," "empty" and the other things they were called by British critics. But he was wise from the start, and he knew also that it was better to have foolish adjectives hurled at his pictures than no adjectives at all, and he put up with them in silence except if a blunder was made, as in the case of *The White Girl*. When the criticism was poisoned and meant to kill, he realized that silence was a mistake, especially as, with his keen vision and extreme sensitiveness, he could see and feel that the critics were carrying the public with them, that gradually he was being laughed *at*, not *with*. He accepted in the same silence the description of that perfect picture of Jo, *The Little White Girl*, as "a bizarre biped,"—bizarre apparently a favorite among his critics' adjectives. But when the vials of ridicule and wrath were poured upon *The Two Little White Girls* he could remain silent no longer. And after the exhibition of that painting in the Royal Academy of 1867, he began to let loose the arrows of his wit until a frightened world shrank in dismay and he gained a new reputation as quarrelsome, a man to whom battle was the spice of life, deliberate in his eccentricity, extravagant in his pose—a charlatan.

II

WHISTLER THE MAN: HIS BITTERNESS

WHISTLER painted the *Two Little White Girls* with, if anything, more than the usual enthusiasm he threw into his work. He wrote of it exultantly, despairingly to Fantin. It was a harmony in color—an Arrangement in White; also a harmony in line—see the wonderful arrangement of the arms of the two figures—*Tiens,* and he made a little sketch of it in his letter. But the harmony bristled with difficulties. He scraped it out, rubbed it out, deplored his training—why could he not have studied under Ingres? and have begun by learning something of drawing?—Of this harmony the critics naturally understood nothing, but to their density he was accustomed. He shrugged his shoulders when Burty—though disappointed that it should be a French critic—discovered irony in the Academy's willingness to hang the picture and regretted the painter's falling away from his early promise. But the English critic Hamerton's pontifical dullness was more than he could bear in silence.

THE MUSIC ROOM, HARMONY IN GREEN AND ROSE,
Freer Collection

Hamerton in the Sixties was already the British arbiter of taste. He dabbled in art to the point of believing himself an authority. At the famous *Salon* of the Refused in 1863 he had laughed with the crowd in front of *The White Girl*, and gloried in it. Now at the Academy in 1867, in front of *The Two Little White Girls, Symphony in White No. 111*, he was too insulted to laugh. *A Symphony in White* indeed? Why, he wrote in *The Saturday Review*, one girl has a yellowish dress and a bit of blue ribbon, the other has a red fan, and, besides, he could see green leaves and flowers. "There is a girl in white on a white sofa, but even this girl has reddish hair, and, of course, there is the flesh color of the complexion." Such stupidity was beyond Whistler's endurance and he let himself go in a letter æons away from the first mild protest of 1863:

"*Bon Dieu!* did this wise person expect white hair and chalked faces? And does he then, in his astounding consequence, believe that a Symphony in F contains no other note, but shall be a continued repetition of F F F? . . . Fool!"

The letter seems to have frightened the editor of *The Saturday Review* and it was not published until many years after. For Whistler it was the opening of the floodgates. He would let no critic subdue his gayety, but to this gayety he gave a new note—a note of raillery, of ridicule, I might have written a note of malice had he not told me once, "I may be wicked, but malicious never!" He was hurt and bitterness was in the gayety. Before the world, he kept up his brave face,—his wicked face. One after another they came now, those wonderful little notes, those wonderful little controversies that he saved from oblivion, or old newspaper files, by collecting them in *The Gentle Art of Making Enemies*. The present generation can scarcely credit the terror they inspired. And the more evident was the terror, the wickeder was the attack. You can see by the twirls and darts of the Butterfly's tail with the sting in it, the signature of these letters, what rollicking fun he was having with "the enemies." The sting grew to be a terror in itself, revealing at a glance the humor of the writer.

By this time whatever Whistler did was twisted into evil or eccentricity in a land where convention rules. The harmless Butterfly created as unspeakable a scandal as his hats and his Harmonies. He used it first in his pictures, and to sign a picture in that fashion simply "was not done" in correct studios. All sorts of meaning were, and are, invented for it that would surprise no one more than Whistler. One ingenious writer recently proved it to be Whistler's portrait. He could have seen only a few Butterflies signed to prints and drawings and letters when he discovered eyes, mouth, nose, even the white lock in the lines. The liveliest imagination could not transform the Butterfly in the paintings into any resemblance to a man's face. The evolution of the Butterfly is simple. It grew out of the interwining of his initials J.M.W. Whistler evolved a Butterfly in which at first the initials were scarcely visible save to the initiated. He was still under the influence of the Japanese and he placed the Butterfly in a little panel, as the Japanese artist placed the inscription on a color print, low in the corner of his picture, or half way up, or wherever it best carried out or fitted into the composition. He sometimes let it wander over the frame which for several years he designed himself. Gradually the Butterfly was freed from Japanese influence until, in the later signatures, it is as hard to find as the initials are in the earlier.

Until the end of the Sixties Whistler had been fairly well treated. Almost every year his pictures and prints had been accepted by the Academy. But the ribaldry of the critics had its effect, and his persistent refusal to paint the fashionable anecdote, to emulate Academicians in searching encyclopedias and classical dictionaries for subjects told against him with Academic juries. When he began to call pictures *Symphonies, Arrangements, Nocturnes,* the limit of Academic patience was reached. Certainly, after the exhibition of the portrait of his

Mother*—*Arrangement in Gray and Black*—in 1872, no painting of his was ever again hung on Academic walls, and it would not have been hung that spring had not Boxall—"the one white man" in the Academic crowd—threatened to resign if it was rejected. The Royal Academy at that period set the standard not only for British artists but for the British public. If Whistler was not Academically recognized, the layman could but ignore him. If the critics jeered aloud, timid artists could venture only to whisper their praise in private.

His contemporaries were unwilling to take him seriously but they could not stop thinking about him, they could not stop talking about him. Everything he did was made public property and, by the Seventies, not one little shred of his private life was left. Everything he did was distorted, exaggerated. He was a man of quick, of violent, temper and gossip spread incredible tales of him as a quarrelsome fellow. Whistler never sought a quarrel, but if forced into one, he fought in dead earnest. Rossetti's limerick was not unwarranted:

There's a combative artist named Whistler
Who is, like his own hog-hairs, a bristler:

* *Note*—It might as well be explained here that Whistler had a way, disconcerting to the cataloguer, of changing his titles. His *Arrangements in Gray and Black* sometimes became *Arrangements in Black*, just as a *Harmony in Flesh Color and Pink* might again figure as *Harmony in Pink and Gray*.

THE WHITE GIRL,
SYMPHONY IN WHITE, NO. I

J. H. Whittemore

A tube of white lead
And a punch on the head
Offer varied attractions to Whistler.

Rossetti's laugh had no malice in it as Whistler
well realized. When, after a quarrel with Seymour
Haden, he was expelled from the Burlington Fine
Arts Club, Gabriel Rossetti and his brother William Michael resigned, both outraged by the way
he had been treated. They knew he was in the
right, and the curious part of it is that Whistler,
with rare exceptions, was in the right. His code was
"If a man gives you the lie to your face, why,
naturally you hit him." The public fancied that he
hit at random, without provocation, out of bad
temper or to set people talking. It was fortunate
for Whistler that, though extremely sensitive, he
had a rare sense of humor—of fun. He felt the un-
justified misunderstanding of himself and his work
but "he always laughed his troubles away." If
people were determined to be fooled, he would fool
them to the top of their bent and, in "surroundings of antagonism," wrap himself in "a species of
misunderstanding." If they wanted to talk, he
would give them something to talk about in good
earnest.

He was never so deliberately outrageous as in
the Seventies and Eighties. Never was his "Ha!
ha!" the laugh at whose sound the timid ran, so

shrill, so penetrating, so far-reaching. He intensified the eccentricities of his dress which hitherto, eccentric as it seemed to others, he had merely adapted to his own taste and comfort. His overcoat grew longer, his hat higher, his cane taller and slimmer. He would go out to dinner without a necktie. The jauntiness of his curls increased. He cultivated the white lock into prominence. When that white lock first appeared there is no exact record. But in the Seventies it was added to his misdemeanors, his eccentricities. Many people have had white locks of the kind without attracting much attention. Whistler's was another public scandal. Its origin was variously explained—it was hereditary, it was the result of the gunfire he was under at the Valparaiso bombardment, it was an affectation, a deliberate eccentricity, and when Whistler knew this was the general opinion, the white lock was more in evidence than before.

It was the same with his daily habits at home. Oftener than not it pleased him to have people about him in the studio; the world said disgraceful, no artist could do honest work before an audience; and Whistler flung the studio door wider open than ever. He loved to entertain, and gossip frowned as if for an artist to entertain was unheard of. He gave Sunday breakfasts, preferring the French hour of noon and French dishes to early, stodgy British breakfasts, and a horrified public denounced

them as foreign, therefore indecent, the worse because the table decorations—the gold fish in a
bowl or the single tall lily—were as unusual.
Worst crime of all was Whistler's habit of keeping
his guests waiting. Lord Wolseley was one of them
on the unspeakable Sunday when he chose the
breakfast hour for his morning bath, his splashing
heard in the drawing-room while Howell kept the
party together by his charm until Whistler appeared, smiling, fresh in white duck, for it was
summer.

If he was late in his own house as host, he was
later as guest in other people's houses, and this was
more unpardonable. Black looks did not disturb
his serenity or modulate the shrill "Ha! ha!" Those
who could edged away from him when they heard
it, dreading to be mixed up in the wickedness of
which it was the prelude. He no longer needed
it for defense when I knew him but of the fear it
inspired I was once the witness—in the Nineties
when Joseph Pennell and I persuaded him to go to
the dinner of the Society of Illustrators of which
he was a Vice-President. There he would be among
a new generation of young men who could appreciate the honor of his presence. He refused to
sit at the high table, it was his first public appearance after his wife's death, and he took a less conspicuous place with Heinemann and ourselves. We
were hardly seated when, to our horror, we saw

Sir James Linton, the President, bringing in Sir Seymour Haden, brother-in-law, and "enemy" beyond redemption. With the soup, Whistler caught sight of Haden. He stuck his monocle in his eye, "Ha! ha!" rang out joyously. Haden gave one frantic look towards us, dropped his spoon, and ran. But this incident helped me to understand the power of that "Ha! ha!" during the two decades when it was a warning and a defense, when Whistler's fortunes were at their lowest ebb and his reputation as charlatan most widely spread.

They were the decades when he was painting one great portrait after another—the *Mother*, the *Carlyle*, the *Miss Alexander*, the *Mrs. Huth*, the *Leyland*, the *Rosa Corder*, the *Lady Archibald Campbell*, the *Lady Meux*, the *Sarasate*. What Englishman of the time who held him in contempt had such a showing to make? It was the period also of the great *Nocturnes*, night rendered in its mystery and loveliness as no painter had ever rendered it before. He knew he was doing good work. When it was passed by and the commonplaces of the popular painter extolled, is it any wonder that he was embittered? And, as if he had not enough to endure from the attitude of the public and the critics, disaster after disaster was leading to the ruin of his private affairs. Indeed, it was disaster all the way through the Seventies.

With the Peacock Room, to which he looked as

THE BALCONY, HARMONY IN FLESH COLOUR AND GREEN
Freer Collection

the beginning of fame and fortune, he lost his best friend and most liberal patron, Frederick Leyland, "the Liverpool Medici," Whistler called him. Leyland bought the *Princesse du Pays de la Porcelaine* and hung it above the mantelpiece in the dining-room of his Prince's Gate Mansion. The decorations of the room clashed with the color scheme of the painting and Whistler suggested alterations in them. One change led to another and when the alterations were finished, in 1877, Whistler had transformed the dining-room into the famous Arrangement of Gold upon Blue, Blue upon Gold—the Peacock Room. All through the summer he worked in a fever of excitement, up at six; the day spent on ladders and scaffoldings, and in hammocks, as he painted walls and ceilings; to bed late with "eyes full of sleep, and peacock feathers." Leyland was away most of the time at Speke Hall, his house by the sea near Liverpool. Whistler's friends—he had a few—were uneasy. What will Leyland say? they asked, had he consulted Leyland?

"Why should I?" was Whistler's answer. "I am doing the most beautiful thing that ever has been done, you know, the most beautiful room."

He gave receptions, issued invitations, held private views. What Leyland thought when he came back he expressed plainly in his check for one thousand pounds, instead of the two thousand guineas Whistler considered his due. Whistler was

furious, really not so much for being paid half the
sum for which he asked as for being paid in pounds.
To the end, few things made him more indignant
than to be given a pound instead of a guinea, the
one little shilling seeming to count for more in his
eyes than the other twenty put together. He had
not finished the decoration on the space of wall
opposite the *Princesse*. He refused to leave the
house until he had. On the blue background he
painted two gold Peacocks, one with claws greedily
clutching the scattered gold coins, the other spread-
ing wide his golden wings in superb and insolent
scorn—"The Rich Peacock and the Poor Peacock,"
Whistler said, and

"You know, there Leyland will sit at dinner, his
back to the *Princesse* and always before him the
Apotheosis of *l'art et l'argent*."

Whistler scored, as he always did but, though a
satisfaction, it was no help out of the difficulties he
was now in head over heels.

Later in the same year, 1877, after the Peacock
Room was finished, Whistler was well represented
in the first exhibition of the Grosvenor Gallery,
invited by Sir Coutts Lindsay, its founder. The fun
poked at his Nocturnes and Arrangements—at his
"materialized spirits and figures in a London fog"
—he let pass lightly. "Ha! ha!" was enough for
that kind of criticism. But another kind to which
he was now subjected he could not and would not

stand. Poor half-mad Ruskin, not long out of one of his periods of retirement—of the nature of which Whistler was in complete ignorance—wrote a notice of the Grosvenor in *Fors Clavigera* for July 2, 1877, in it the often-quoted sentence:

"For Mr. Whistler's own sake, no less than for the protection of the purchaser, Sir Coutts Lindsay ought not to have admitted works in the gallery in which the ill-educated conceit of the artist so nearly approached the aspect of willful imposture. I have seen and heard much of cockney impudence before now; but never expected to hear a coxcomb ask two hundred guineas for flinging a pot of paint in the public's face."

"Sounds rather like libel," George Boughton said to Whistler the afternoon he had the pleasure of reading this at the Arts Club.

"Well—that I shall try to find out," said Whistler, and he did at the Trial, as momentous an event in his career as the Peacock Room and the opening of the Grosvenor Gallery.

In anticipation the Trial was "nuts and nectar" to Ruskin, "the greatest lark for a long time in the Courts," to Charles Keene who should have known better. In court, however, it was Whistler who scored again. He won his case. He made Judge, Counsel and witnesses ridiculous. But the triumph was ruinous. Artists were mostly on the other side. Judgment was given for him without costs, dam-

ages were valued at a farthing. At once a collection
was taken up to pay the costs of Ruskin who could
well afford to pay them himself. For Whistler, pen
niless, there was no collection, only the suggestion
He laughed this trouble too away. "In the even
of a subscription," he wrote his solicitor, "I would
willingly contribute my own mite."

All the same, he realized how little of a laughing
matter it was. By this time his affairs were in a
hopeless mess. The Peacock Room had left him one
thousand guineas poorer than he expected to be
The Trial, though he won, added to his debts. And
as luck would have it, shortly before, encouraged
by the sale of some of his pictures, the invitation
to exhibit in the Grosvenor, and the expectation or
promise of students, he had undertaken to build
a house in which he would have his first real studio
—the White House. He was therefore facing
unusually heavy expenses. It was inevitable that
the next court in which he found himself should
be the Bankruptcy Court.

His debts kept on multiplying and creditors
were alarmed. Architects and builders were not
working for nothing. Greengrocers and fishmon-
gers pursued him with bills. Tax collectors were
about. He kept borrowing money, here, there, ev-
erywhere, pawning his pictures, getting out his
printing press and going back to etching, trying
lithography for the first time. Bailiffs in the house

THE LITTLE WHITE GIRL, SYMPHONY IN WHITE, NO. 2
With Permission of the National Gallery, London

became a matter of course. And, as far as the world could see, his gayety had seldom been so unrestrained. One might have thought the bailiffs were provided to amuse his guests. He disguised them as butlers at his Sunday breakfasts—"liveried attendants"—they had to be put to some use, he explained.

"Wonderful fellows," he told his breakfast party one Sunday, "you will see how excellently they wait at table and to-morrow, you know, well, if you want, you can see them sell the chairs you sit on every bit as well. Amazing!"

"Your servants seem to be extremely attentive," a guest said to him another Sunday.

"Oh, yes," said Whistler, "I assure you they wouldn't leave me."

To the bailiff who asked to be paid because of his own financial misfortunes, Whistler's answer was "Ha! ha! you must have a man in yourself, you know."

When the time of the sale approached he wrote to the people he invited to Sunday breakfast that they would know the house by the bills stuck up on it. He rebelled only when the posters were hung without sufficient care. When he saw them loosened by rain, flapping in the wind, he roused the bailiff though it was midnight, made him fetch a ladder and paste them down securely. He would not put up with slovenliness as long as he was living in the

house. He took the meetings of creditors as if they
were got up for his delight. He was but more dan-
dified as the money to pay for dandyism vanished.
His coat seemed to grow longer than ever, his hat
higher, his curls curlier, his monocle more startling.
"Ha! ha!" was his greeting. "Well, you know, here
I am in the City."

Inextinguishable his laughter, but those who
knew Whistler knew the keen suffering it disguised.
He was declared a bankrupt in May, 1879, he was
sold out, he had not a penny in the world, and he
laughed.

The Fine Art Society came to the rescue with a
commission for twelve etchings in Venice. He left
in his studio, in anticipation of the sale, three cruel
caricatures of Leyland, one the horrible but beautiful *Filthy Lucre,* or *The Gold Scab,* the "Liverpool Medici" breaking out in an eruption of gold
as he sits at his piano, the bitterest caricature an
artist ever imagined, now in the collection of Mrs.
Spreckels. Over his front door he wrote: "Except
the Lord build the house, they labor in vain that
build it. E. W. Godwin, F.S.A., built this one."
Then he packed up his copper plates and started
for Venice in the autumn of 1879. His troubles pursued him. He heard of the disappearance of pictures
that the Bankruptcy sale could not account for, the
Fine Art Society wrote indignantly when the etchings were not done on time—as if Whistler could

have done anything on time, indifferent to the quality of what he was doing. He was desperately poor, so poor he would say he was living on "cat's meat and cheese parings." Heaven knows what would have become of him if Maud, the model who now replaced Jo, had not hurried down to Venice to look after him, to pose for him, to cook for him, to see to the comfort so essential to him when he worked, and in the social distraction as essential to his well-being, getting up frugal feasts to which he could summon his friends. At least Venice was refreshingly free of "the enemies." He was among friends. The Brownings, Curtises and Bronsons who were residents, could appreciate him, their palace doors were open to him. The town was full of artists who believed in his art, asked nothing better than to be with him. Duveneck and "Duveneck's boys" had come up from Florence. Venetian and Spanish artists were as sympathetic. It was like a revival of the old *Quartier Latin* life, talks over dinner in friendly little restaurants or, when he could not afford it, in his own place, talks over coffee at the Quadri or Florian's in the Piazza, at the Orientale on the Riva. It was a life he loved. And he never worked harder. His etchings of Venice and his Venice pastels were made during these months. Once he finished them, he had finished with Venice. He knew that for the artist who is not a native, too long a stay in Venice is death. He did not run the risk that for a while threatened ruin to Duveneck's art, perhaps accomplished it.

Late in 1880 Whistler returned to London. "The Islanders," his name for the English, must have drawn a long sigh of relief at his departure, no longer going in fear of the dreaded "Ha! ha!" And then, suddenly, without warning, wickeder than ever, wearing a Venetian overcoat with three capes that would have sent shivers through Sackville Street, acquiring a dog to lend the last bewildering touch, he reappeared in London, in Bond Street, at the Fine Art Society's. Here he found an exhibition of Twelve Great Etchers, a press in the Gallery and Goulding printing.

"Well, you know, I was just home," was the story as he told it to me, "nobody had seen me, and I drove up in a landau. Nobody expected me. In one hand I held my long cane, with the other I led by a ribbon a beautiful little white Pomeranian dog; it too had turned up suddenly. As I walked in I spoke to no one but, putting up my glass, I looked at the prints on the walls! 'Dear me! Dear me!' I said. 'Still the same old sad work. Dear me!' And Haden was there, talking hard to Brown and laying down the law, and as he said 'Rembrandt,' I said 'Ha! ha!' and he vanished and then—"

There was the Whistler London knew in the Eighties—doing the unexpected cruelly, dressing the part extraordinarily, tormenting a conventional

THOMAS CARLYLE,
ARRANGEMENT IN GREY AND BLACK, NO. 2

Corporation Art Gallery, Glasgow

public shockingly, and dropping his "Ha! ha's!"
like bombs in their midst. Not that his troubles
were at an end. Far from it. He was as desperately
poor as in Venice. He at first took a bare barn of a
studio in the Fulham Road, he and Maud living
close by in an unpretending little cottage which he
called the Pink Palace. M. Théodore Duret was
having his portrait painted to test Whistler's theory
that a man should be painted in the clothes of his
period, however hopeless, that color could be got
even out of modern evening dress. When Duret
went for a sitting and to dine afterwards with
Whistler and Maud, he would carry a bottle of
wine in one pocket and some fruit or cake in another, sure beforehand of the bareness of their
larder. For the first few years nobody commissioned a portrait save Lady Meux who should be
remembered for her independence, her daring and
her appreciation, even if she could treat him to
occasional polite Billingsgate. Whistler exhibited
his Twelve Etchings at the Fine Art Society's. To
the critics they were "another crop of Whistler's
little jokes." A year later he exhibited his pastels
in the same Gallery, decorating it, making it an
Arrangement in Gold and Brown, for he believed
that beautiful work should be beautifully shown.
The public shrieked, rocked with laughter. Somebody at the Private View asked the price of a pastel:

"Sixty guineas? Why, that's enormous!"

Whistler always heard everything, especially what he was not intended to hear.

"Ha! ha! Enormous!" he laughed in his turn. "Why, not at all. I can assure you it took me quite half an hour to do it—" a reëcho of the Trial, this.

One day at the door of the Gallery he met a patron of art and his wife coming out from the exhibition, both looking bored to death. At sight of him the patron chuckled, shook hands warmly.

"We have both been looking at your things and have been so much amused."

"And," said Whistler to me years afterwards, "I laughed with him. I always did with people of that kind, and then they said I was not serious."

Another exhibition of etchings—the second Venetian series—was held, again at the Fine Art Society's, in 1883, the Gallery this time an Arrangement in Yellow and White, the Catalogue a rare mixture of Whistler's gayety and seriousness. Below the title of each print he quoted from some unfortunate critic's pronouncement in the past. Or here is his own description in a letter to Waldo Story:

"I take, my dear Waldo, all that I have collected of the silly drivel of the wise fools who write, and I pepper and salt it about the catalogue . . . in short, I put their nose to the grindstone and turn the wheel with a whir! I give 'em Hell! quoting old Solomon about the fool to my heart's content. The whole thing is a joy—and indeed a masterpiece of mischief."

On the title page he printed the text: "Out of their own mouths shall ye judge them."

The next year, 1884, the exhibition was chiefly of water-colors, at Dowdeswell's. The Gallery was an *Arrangement in Flesh Color and Gray,* a new affectation to the critics, another offense to the public, though the public crowded to be offended every time. Whistler's report of the Pastel Exhibition was: "Bond Street BLOCKED. All traffic suspended. No. Amazing!"

Whistler did his best to encourage the bewilderment. At the *Yellow and White* Exhibition he wore yellow socks and his attendants, yellow neckties. Little yellow and white butterflies were distributed. He wrote the details to Waldo Story: "Fancy the Princess [the Princess of Wales] with the Butterfly! Amazing—and Lady Archie [Archibald Campbell] with one on her shoulder and one on her hat." According to an interviewer, Sir Edmund Gosse went home from the Gallery with the Golden Butterfly perched on the summit of his top hat conspicuously, and he all unconscious of its presence there. This was in the days when pretentious painters showed their work in solemn galleries draped with heavy red velvet, lit by artificial light, rows of chairs in front of the masterpiece for the worshipers, leaflets of explanation distributed at the door. How could the artist be accepted as serious who chose to appear in fantastic dress, top hat dipped low over his nose, tight-fitting frock coat, long wand-like cane, pink bows on his pumps—or so it was said—in a gallery filled with light and color and joyousness? Absurdity in his costume, absurdity in his work, absurdity in the decoration of his exhibition gallery—deliberate absurdity, that is what people said. Whistler has his revenge now that he is hailed as master and his scheme for the arrangement of an exhibition is almost universally adopted.

In the midst of the general misunderstanding, little straws began to show the observant man which way the wind was presently to blow. A younger generation was arising who did not accept their Gospel from the Academy. A group of young men began to gather about Whistler. They saw beyond the long cane, the white lock, the three-decked cape of his overcoat, the hat tipped over his eye, beyond that still more extraordinary combination of the same un-English hat and wand-like cane with long black frock coat, white waistcoat and white trousers. They understood. As every master does in time, he drew to him devoted disciples. The public still howled, the Academy was still scornful, but the Society of British Artists begged him to join as member and shortly elected him their President. The Society had not then, has

CICELY HENRIETTA, MISS ALEXANDER,
HARMONY IN GREY AND GREEN
With Permission of the National Gallery, London

not now, a great reputation, his Presidency ended soon enough to the renewed jeering of public and Academicians. But the incident brought a ray of light in the darkness of misunderstanding. The dawn of recognition was not far off.

III

WHISTLER THE ARTIST: HIS SERIOUSNESS

AS Whistler was the gayest of men, so was he the most serious of artists, and not to realize the fact is to fail to appreciate him. From the beginning those two opposing sides of his character were equally in evidence. Those who knew him as a child remembered the high spirits that disturbed his mother no more vividly than the pencil that was forever in his hand. An old friend of Whistler's, a Mrs. Livermore, was living when Joseph Pennell and I first began to collect material for his Life and the pencil figures in the earliest memories she had for us. When she called on Mrs. Whistler shortly after the birth of "Willy"—Dr. Whistler— "Jemmie" was not to be found.

"I went softly about the room until I saw a very small form prostrate and at full length on the shelf under the dressing table, and I took hold of an arm and a leg and placed him on my knee, and then said, 'What were you doing, dear, under the table?' 'I'se drawing,' and in one very beautiful little hand he held the paper, in the other the pencil."

The story is continued in Mrs. Whistler's Diary of the St. Petersburg days. Her notes were not only of the scrapes her excitable boy got into, but of his delight in fine pictures, his despair over the loss of a drawing lesson in school, his eagerness to start for his classes at the Academy of Fine Arts after his admission there as student. One evening Sir William Allen, "the great Scotch artist" in his time and to-day forgotten, was taking tea with the Whistlers and the talk turned to a picture he was painting.

"This made Jemmie's eyes express so much interest that his love for art was discovered, and Sir William must needs see his attempts. When my boys said good-night, the great artist remarked to me, 'Your little boy has uncommon genius, but do not urge him beyond his inclinations.' I told him his gift had only been cultivated as an amusement, and that I was obliged to interfere, or his application would confine him more than we approved."

Whistler already suffered from rheumatism in the St. Petersburg years. One winter he was kept in bed several weeks by an unusually severe attack.

"What a blessing," his mother writes, "is such a contented temper as his, so grateful for every kindness and rarely complains. He is now enjoying a huge volume of Hogarth's engravings, so famous in the Gallery of Artists. We put the immense book on the bed, and draw the great easy chair close up, so that he can feast upon it without fatigue. He said, while so engaged yesterday, 'Oh, how I wish I were well; I want so to show these engravings to my drawing-master; it is not every one who has a chance of seeing Hogarth's own engravings of his originals'; and then added in his own happy way 'and if I had not been ill, mother, perhaps no one would have thought of showing them to me.' "

It was the same story over again in Pomfret, in West Point, in the Coast Survey office. Pen, pencil and etching needle kept him busy, in all places, at all hours, in all seasons—always. Whatever else he might neglect, he never grudged a minute to art. As a Cadet he was at the head in drawing, however near the tail in his other classes. He might show an uncadetlike levity at drill or in barracks, but never at the drawing lesson. He already had an appreciation of his own aims and methods and their rightness. He was indignant when Robert W. Weir, the master, not content to criticize, attempted to correct or improve his work. When he saw Weir one day coming with a brush freshly filled with India ink, Whistler shielded his drawing with his hand and begged "Oh, don't, sir, don't! You'll spoil it."

The tradition of his gayety lingered in Paris— the gayety of the Idle Apprentice. The record of his seriousness as artist is in the work he did there as student. He already proved in the life he lived what he afterwards expressed in words, "Art and joy go

VALPARAISO BAY, NOCTURNE IN BLUE AND GOLD,
Freer Collection

together." When he danced with Finette and Fumette at the balls in the *Quartier* everybody saw that he danced with enthusiasm. What everybody did not see was the greater enthusiasm, the greater concentration with which he etched the portraits of his partners. He loafed in *cafés and restaurants* with Drouet the sculptor and Becquet the musician, but they had to pay for his friendship by posing for him, and there was no *blague*, no *farce*, in posing for Whistler. He ran up bills for breakfasts and dinners at Lalouette's restaurant and settled for them, with good interest compounded, in the fame of his etching of Bibi Lalouette, the daughter of the house. Wherever he went, whatever his mission, somebody had to pose: Delâtre, the printer, Riault, the engraver, Bibi Valentin, child of another engraver, Astruc, editor of *L'Artiste*. The greater the lark, the richer the harvest. The greatest lark of all was his tramp to Alsace with Ernest Delannoy, the complete Bohemian Whistler was supposed to be. *Impayable*, was George Meredith's word for Whistler's story of this tramp and their adventures when their money ran out and they had to draw the peasants and innkeepers by the way for food and lodging, or go hungry and sleep in the straw. It was the season of autumn fairs and in despair they joined a lady who played the trombone and a gentleman who played the violin and the four gave performances of "two arts" for a few sous. But from this vagabond tramp Whistler brought back to Paris most of the etchings published in *The French Set,* now the envy of artists, an investment for dealers and collectors. Had the myth of the Idle Apprentice never been invented, the talk would have been of the seriousness of the American student in Paris.

The myth crossed the Channel with Whistler—too irrepressibly gay as a man to be serious as an artist, was London's verdict; London's gossip, all of his frivolity, his audacities, his impertinences, never of his sincerity, earnestness and industry. The truth is in his work and, if that did not remain, his letters to Fantin would still be a record of his struggles, his wrestling with technical problems, his despair, his hope, his exultation with success, his agony with failure. *"Ah! mon cher, comme il a du travailler,"* was a cry from his heart when he wrote urging Fantin to join him at Biarritz for the often proposed and never accomplished journey to study Velasquez at Madrid. He knew what the diligence of the master must have been—what the toiling always of genius before perfection can be attained. Could Ruskin have seen these letters he would have marveled at the effort and the study and the scrupulous care that went to flinging a pot of paint in the public's face. Again and again "the coxcomb" reproaches himself for that early indifference to Ingres from whom, after all, the principles of sound drawing were to be learned. Again and again he reproaches himself for his devotion to Courbet and his preoccupation with *ce damné Réalisme*. Not really that Courbet ever influenced him, he was sure, he was too personal in his art for that, too rich in qualities that were not Courbet's. Still the cry of Nature had appealed to him and he had copied her, with the vanity of *l'écolier débauché*. Letter after letter revealed the earnestness of his purpose and his method—an astounding series, but for Fantin alone. Whistler had not yet begun the letters intended for the public and the pamphlets he later collected together in *The Gentle Art of Making Enemies*—the Bible he called it, and not without reason. It is the Bible of Art to all who read with intelligence.

The first public pronouncement that astonished the world by its revelation of the serious Whistler was given at the Trial. His dignity disappointed Judge and Counsel who were prepared for a farce, and the crowd who had come to laugh. One answer in his cross-examination has been and is continually quoted, and much mangled in the quoting. It was led up to by the question of the Attorney-General, Counsel for the Defendant:

"Can you tell me how long it took you to knock off that Nocturne?

"*Whistler:* I beg your pardon? (Laughter.)

"*Attorney-General:* I am afraid that I am using a

term that applies rather perhaps to my own work. . . .

"*Whistler:* Let us say then, how long did I take to 'knock off'—I think that is it—to knock off that Nocturne; well, as well as I remember, about a day. . . . I may have still put a few more touches to it the next day if the painting were not dry. I had better say, then, that I was two days at work on it.

"*Attorney-General:* The labor of two days then, is that for which you ask two hundred guineas?

"*Whistler:* No, I ask it for the knowledge of a lifetime."

The whole Trial was such a misapprehension, such a determination to see farce in the practice of art, to Whistler the most serious thing on this earth, examination and cross-examination afforded him such a slight opportunity to say all he thought should be said, though what he did say made a deep impression, that a month after the Trial he published the first of his little brown-paper covered pamphlets: *Whistler* v. *Ruskin: Art and Art Critics*. It is a denunciation not solely of Ruskin, but of the whole tribe of critics who do harm and not good. Whistler's words explain his creed more eloquently than anybody else could explain it for him:

"Over and over again did the Attorney-General cry out aloud, in the agony of his cause, 'what is

OLD BATTERSEA BRIDGE, NOCTURNE IN BLUE AND GOLD, *Tate Gallery*

to become of painting if the critics withhold their lash?'

"As well might he ask what is to become of mathematics under similar circumstances, were they possible. I maintain that two and two the mathematician would continue to make four, in spite of the whine of the amateur for three, or the cry of the critic for five. We are told that Mr. Ruskin has devoted his long life to art, and as a result is 'Slade Professor' at Oxford. In the same sentence, we have thus his position and its worth. It suffices not, *Messieurs!* a life passed among pictures makes not a painter—else the policeman in the National Gallery might assert himself. As well allege that he who lives in a library must needs die a poet. Let not Mr. Ruskin flatter himself that mere education makes the difference between himself and the policeman when both stand gazing in the Gallery. . . .

"What a commerce it all is, to be sure!

"No sham in it either!—no 'bigod nonsense.' They [the critics] are all 'doing good'—yes, they all do good to Art. Poor Art! what a sad state the slut is in, and these gentlemen shall help her. The artist alone, by the way, is to no purpose, and remains unconsulted; his work is explained and rectified without him, by the one who was never in it —but upon whom God—always good, though sometimes careless, has thrown away the knowledge refused to the author—poor devil! . . .

"Art is joyously received as a matter of opinion; and that it should be based upon laws as rigid and defined as those of the known sciences, is a supposition no longer to be tolerated by modern cultivation."

And then he draws the parallel, exposes the absurdity:

"The Observatory at Greenwich under the direction of an Apothecary! The College of Physicians with Tennyson as President! and we know that madness is about. But a school of art with an accomplished *littérateur* at its head disturbs no one! and is actually what the world receives as rational, while Ruskin writes for pupils, and Colvin holds forth at Cambridge."

Whistler was in dead earnest. He was upholding the truth he never ceased to maintain, that art is a science—the science of the beautiful. Of course the critics did not approve of the pamphlet—did not follow his argument, did not agree with his conclusion. Tom Taylor, Civil Servant and, in his leisure moments, art authority of *The Times,* who had been writing nonsense about Velasquez and been exposed by Whistler, involved himself still further by attempting to prove Whistler wrong. Whistler answered with the joyous laugh that always convinced the public of his hopeless frivolity, in art as in life:

"Shrive your naughty soul and give up Velasquez, and pass your last days properly in the Home Office. . . . Set your house in order with the Government for arrears of time and paper, and leave vengeance to the Lord, who will forgive my 'garbling' Tom Taylor's writing."

Tom Taylor wrote again, a letter Whistler did well to preserve in *The Gentle Art* as a typical example of the critical treatment to which he was for long subjected, the reason of his gay but bitter wit, his relentless persecution of his critics:

"Pardon me, my dear Whistler, for having taken you *au sérieux* even for a moment.

"I ought to have remembered that your penning, like your painting, belongs to the region of chaff."

"Why, my dear old Tom," was Whistler's answer, "I never *was* serious with you, even when you were among us. Indeed, I killed you quite, as who should say, without seriousness, 'A rat! A rat!' you know, rather cursorily."

I have quoted liberally from the pamphlet and the ensuing correspondence because nothing else in *The Gentle Art,* that is, no one incident, shows so well the contrast between Whistler serious and Whistler gay—Whistler refusing to overlook any want of respect to art and Whistler exposing with biting humor the ignorance of an unfortunate critic—the contrast that has not wholly ceased to confuse the world.

Whistler was also serious in his *Ten O'Clock,* a

profession of faith convincing in its sincerity, a
work of art perfect as his portraits and his Nocturnes. And he was serious in his *Propositions*, his
statement of technical truths, the truths that ruled
him in his own practice and that are an unfailing
guide to etchers and painters. To turn to these
Propositions to-day is to be amazed at their fresh-
ness and their vigor. They help to establish his con-
tention that only the artist is qualified to write of
art. *Propositions* and *Ten O'Clock* survive while
the outpourings of Hamerton, Tom Taylor and the
others have quietly passed away.

To hear Whistler talk of art with sympathetic
friends was to be left without a doubt of his profound seriousness. Because his subjects in London
and Venice and Paris were usually streets, shops,
the river and its shipping, and the out-of-the-way
canal, an old doorway, a crumbling wall in prefer-
ence to the great monuments of the past, it was
concluded that for these monuments he had no
appreciation, no admiration, that he disdained them
because they were difficult. Whistler always said it
was an impertinence to reproduce the masterpieces
of the masters. And, besides, for his purpose he
sought his own subjects as the masters had sought
theirs. You could not listen to him when old masters and masterpieces were discussed and not be
convinced of the reverence in which he held them.
That old story of his comment "Why drag in Ve-

THE FALLING ROCKET, NOCTURNE IN BLACK AND GOLD
Mrs. S. Untermeyer

lasquez?" in answer to some silly person's silly joke,
has been repeated over and over again as an in-
stance not of his amusement in gulling his critics
which was what it meant, but of his vanity and
indifference to all art save his own. We wonder
now how this could have been thought or suggested of the artist who wrote of the "Master of
Madrid" as he "who towers above all," whose brush,
dipped in light and air "made his people live
within their frames, and *stand upon their legs,* that
all nobility and sweetness and tenderness and mag-
nificence should be theirs by right."

Art is rare, every man who calls himself an artist
is not to be accepted. But before the chosen, before
the true masters no one was more sincere in his
homage than Whistler. One of my most memorable
experiences was of my visit with him to the National Gallery just after his wife's death, when his
grief could not kill his joy in Velasquez and Titian,
above all in Tintoretto's *Milky Way,* a painting his
wife had loved. They helped him forget, as long
as he was in the Gallery he was absorbed in the
splendor of the masterpieces on the walls. No two
painters could be further apart in method and
manner than Tintoretto and Whistler. But he was
not therefore blind to beauty of strong color and
flamboyant design. I remember too his interest
when Ochtervelt's *Lady Standing at a Spinet* was
shown in the Winter Exhibition of Old Masters

at the Royal Academy in 1902. Ochtervelt was then all but unknown in London. Whistler had gone to the Academy, weak and wretched as he was, especially to see it and the Kingston Lacy *Las Meniñas*, and that evening, dining with us, it seemed as if he had taken a new lease of life when he talked about the Ochtervelt and its beauty of surface, for "the finish, the delicacy, the elegance" of the Dutch masters like Terborch and Vermeer enchanted him. I remember his talk of Claude Lorraine, his comparisons between the work of the French master, full of knowledge, and the work of Turner," "the old amateur," and he would take Joseph Pennell to the National Gallery and, in front of those paintings of Claude and Turner that hang there side by side, point out the accomplishment in the one and the bungling in the other. It is curious how Turner could have made the hanging together a condition of his gift, so entirely does this arrangement result in his own discomfiture. George Sauter was in the Haarlem Gallery with Whistler shortly after the illness which was almost his end during the summer of 1902 and told us of Whistler's raptures over Franz Hals' group of old women, the painting of the flesh, the quality of those wonderful blacks and whites.—"Oh, what a swell he was—can you see it all?—and the character—how he rendered it?" They were alone in the place, the Guardian had let them stay on after closing time and Whistler, mounted on a chair, the better to study the technique, moved his fingers very tenderly over the face of one of the old women—"Oh, I must touch it—just for the fun of it."

This hardly sounds as if Whistler disdained all art save his own. The truth is that he disdained no art in which there was beauty and, indeed, he could not conceive of art without beauty, without distinction, without refinement. To him art was a science, its one and only end to deal in beauty. We have got beyond so simple a theory to-day when artists' talk is all of self-expression. I can fancy Whistler's laugh at this talk as if they had suddenly made a new discovery and it had not been the desire, the irrepressible necessity of the artist to express himself ever since his struggles over his first decorated pot and first drawings on the walls of his cave. The difference is that until the coming of the "modernists" the artist believed that this expression of himself should be made in terms of beauty. Moreover, he believed that his success depended on his mastery of his tools. Whistler was carrying on the only right tradition of art when he strove for beauty in his work and knowledge in his technique. For the artist who could not express himself in terms of art—in beauty of line, of color, of tone, of drawing—Whistler would have shown no mercy, seeing clearly that the language of art was for no man who had not mastered these terms, however wonderful, or powerful, or ambitious might be the self that sought expression.

Artists associated with him, under his Presidency, either in the Society of British Artists, or in the International, would be the first to insist upon the seriousness of his aims and methods. Outsiders jeered when he presided over the British Artists, but that was in the Eighties and was still the fashion. The International was started towards the end of the next decade when the tide had turned, and whatever of the old contempt might survive was kept decorously out of sight. His aim in each Society was, by the dignity of its conduct and its exhibitions, to uphold the dignity of art. He worked hard to this end with Council and members, in his official capacity allowing no familiarity. He was the symbol, as it were, of the Society and by his conduct he would make its high standard clear. It was a revelation to the many who thought the British Artists had chosen a clown to sit in the Presidential chair. The few were prepared for both the high standard and his determination to maintain it. The rank and file of the British Artists, however, much preferred comfortable mediocrity and when they learned, as they did quickly, that Whistler had no intention to encourage it, they rebelled. His position became impossible and he resigned, the minority, the men of promise and performance, resigning

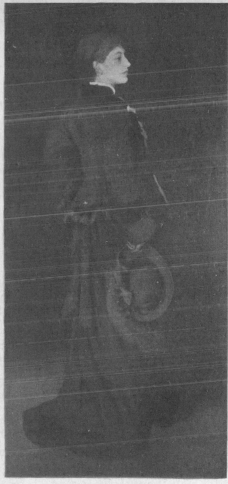

MISS ROSA CORDER,
ARRANGEMENT IN BLACK AND BROWN
Frick Gallery

with him. It was a moment for laughter, and
Whistler laughed: "The Artists came out," he said,
"and the British remained," and he congratulated
the Society on no longer being able to say that they
had the right man in the wrong place.

By the time the International was founded the
British had been forced to admit that the clown
was an artist after all. He had devoted friends
among the younger men, none more staunch in
his devotion than Joseph Pennell. The members of
the Glasgow School, Guthrie, Lavery and the others,
had from the beginning looked up to him as master
and now accepted him as President. The members
of the New English Art Club, or rather the loyal
among them, gathered about him. He was the
leader of the strongest opposition or secession London had ever seen and, had it not been for his illness and death when the Society was but a few
years old, the power of the International with the
younger generation would have made it more than
the rival it had already become to the Royal
Academy, and ceased to be after his death.

His students never disputed his seriousness. The
scheme of a school in the White House came to
nothing, thanks to Ruskin. But about the same
time that the International was founded in London,
the Académie Carmen, with Whistler as master and
regular visitor, was established in Paris. It suffered,

as the International suffered, from his illness during his last years. In the winter he was often confined to the house, or else he went where the climate
was kinder and less harsh than in London and
Paris. His absence led inevitably to disappointment,
grumbling and dwindling of numbers, until finally
in the winter of 1901, which he was spending in
Corsica, the school was closed. He had had time to
make his influence felt, to have innumerable stories
told of him and his visits, and, from beginning
to end, to impress his sincerity and seriousness upon
every one connected with the experiment. He was
there "to teach the surface application of paint and
brushes" and he required seriousness equal to his
in all who came to acquire the knowledge he could
impart. He was to be received as a master, not as a
good fellow in shirt-sleeves. He had his theories,
his methods, his principles of technique. And,
astonishing as it may seem, Whistler, the Idle Apprentice, supposed to have paid no attention to his
master, Gleyre, remembered what he learned at
Gleyre's, not only in his own painting, but in his
teaching. Gleyre taught that the color scheme
should be arranged on the palette before the painting was begun on canvas, he insisted that ivory
black was the base of tone. And so did Whistler
at the Académie. This was the reason of the little
verse that went the rounds of the studio:

I bought a palette just like his,
  His colors and his brush.
The devil of it is, you see,
  I did not buy his touch.

Students, accustomed to the ways of other studios, were mystified by the dignity and decorum
demanded at the Académie Carmen, and it must
be admitted that many of the innumerable stories
that came of it are funny. There was the man in
the men's class whom Whistler found with a pipe
in his mouth at the hour of the master's visit.
"Really," said Whistler, "you had better stop painting for you might get interested in your work and
your pipe would go out." There was the plaintive
young lady who, when he did not approve of her
work, thought that he wanted her to paint what
she saw. "Yes," he said, "and the shock will come
when you see what you paint." There was the pretentious amateur whom Whistler asked, "Have
you been through college? I suppose you shoot?
Fish, of course? Go in for football, no doubt? Yes?
Well, then, I can let you off from painting."

However freely stories circulated among the
students, when he appeared they were as serious
as their master, sometimes too nervous and frightened to profit by his visit. He knew how to inspire
respect. People might misinterpret his "Ha! ha!"
But his students could not mistake his seriousness

as artist and master. And, when they showed they had anything in them, Whistler, by his interest, quickly put an end to the first nervousness in his presence.

In fact, the people, young or old, who saw Whistler intimately, those who worked with or under him, never wavered in their conviction of his intense seriousness, his humility before his "Goddess," his sympathy with all as sincere as himself in her service. He was the pretender, the buffoon in art solely to the docile public of a highly conventional age in a country which is the headquarters of convention.

THE YELLOW BUSKIN,
LADY ARCHIBALD CAMPBELL
ARRANGEMENT IN BLACK
Wilstach Collection, Philadelphia

IV

WHISTLER THE ARTIST: HIS PAINTINGS

WHISTLER used to tell his students that he could teach them how to paint, but only God Almighty could make artists of them. He also taught, in and out of the Académie, that the important business of the artist is to carry on tradition, not to undertake self-consciously to be original.

In his own case God Almighty had interfered. Whistler was an artist and the fact revealed itself in his work from the beginning. What, according to his own theory, it was his business to do, he did. He had no desire, like the wholesale modern revolutionary, to smash our heirloom of masterpieces and to start out anew like a little child or the savage in the jungle. He was a man of too great common sense, his love of beauty was too strong a passion. To him it would have been a crime to attempt to rid ourselves of our heritage from earlier generations. He studied the work of the past wherever and whenever he had the chance. He copied it in the Louvre in what is now considered an out-of-date fashion. Instead of making light of the knowledge and achievement of the Old Masters, he took from them all they had to give and then, God Almighty having made him an artist, developed something essentially his own, something that stamped him as the rare genius of his or any time.

His first pictures, done in his Paris student days, show him the rival of Stevenson as the "sedulous ape." It has been said of them before, but is worth saying again, that they "smell of the Louvre." The *Mère Gérard*, the *Head of the Old Man Smoking*, his own portrait—*Whistler in the Big Hat*—suggest hours of humility and intelligent observation in that great gallery, many spent before Rembrandt —the Rembrandt who has grown with the years more somber, more mysterious, deeper in tone. And yet, already in these early Whistlers, *Arrangements in Black* before he invented the name, there is something of the matured Whistler in the placing of the subject on the canvas, the treatment of the blacks, the feeling for design unusual in the student who seldom aims higher than to make as exact a copy of the model as possible, with what little skill he can muster in the drawing and the modeling. The something different in Whistler is developed still further in his next painting, *At the Piano*, or *The Piano Picture* as it was once better known. Here, the striving after design, composition, is much more evident in the grouping of the two figures; in the way Lady Haden's black gown, as she

sits playing, balances the short white skirts of little
Annie who stands by the piano her arm resting
upon it; in the use made of the contrast between
the curves of the gowns and the straight lines of
the piano, the dado, the picture frames on the
wall. Whistler had begun to consider not merely
the portrait, but the relation of his sitters to the
canvas they had to fill, the harmony in line and
color of which they were the motive. To examine
the picture attentively is to wonder that a student
should have attained so high a degree of accomplishment and to understand why Courbet was
struck with it in Bonvin's studio.

Courbet, rejected that very year, 1859, at the
first International Exhibition, was holding a show
of his own and issuing his first *Manifesto*. As long
as young men study art, there must and will be
an opposition, and the Prophet of Realism was just
the painter to be chosen as leader of the new opposition by students who had had enough of Roman-
ticism. Whistler did not see much of Courbet while
he was studying in Paris. Some one took him once
to Courbet's studio and he was deeply impressed,
saying, as he walked away, *"C'est un grand artiste!
C'est un grand artiste!"* But after the Bonvin exhibition student and master were brought into
more intimate relations. They were together, Jo
also of the company, in Brittany, on the coast, in
the summer of 1861, when Whistler painted *Alone*

with the Tide, unquestionably under Courbet's influence. The winter of 1861-62 Whistler spent in Paris, his studio in the Boulevard des Batignolles, Jo posing for *The White Girl.* Courbet came to see them there, Jo's beautiful red hair a powerful attraction, and in his portraits of her, *La Belle Irlandaise* and *Jo, Femme d'Irlande,* he made the most of the hair but missed the sad pale beauty of the face. As he saw her, she is a curiously buxom Jo to have inspired Swinburne's poem *Before the Mirror*—that, however, was later on—Courbet did not go with Whistler and Jo to Biarritz in the summer of 1862, but his influence did and is unmistakable in *The Blue Wave,* also in pictures painted in London during this period—*The Last of Old Westminster, The Music Room.* It was the period for which Whistler, afterwards writing to Fantin, could not find words indignant enough—the period when "that damned realism" had him in its grip. But under the influence of Courbet, as under the influence of the Louvre, Whistler could not efface, subordinate himself. In that lovely *Music Room,* as in *At the Piano,* you find the same arrangement of black and white in the tall figure in riding habit who fills the center of the canvas and little Annie Haden always in white muslin, and again there is the same balance in the curving lines of the dresses and straight lines of dado and picture frames. And there is besides a tender delicate ren-

PABLO SARASATE,
ARRANGEMENT IN BLACK,
Carnegie Institute

dering of the flowered chintz curtains and a sub-
ordination of detail to the painter's harmony, that
mark already a great advance and foretell his coming complete emancipation from Courbet and his
discovery that "Nature is very rarely right, to such
an extent even, that it might almost be said that
Nature is usually wrong." Whistler was not content
to paint an exact copy of his sitters and the details of their dress and surroundings. In his vision
of beauty, art touched reality with its magic.
Already, while he was painting in the Boulevard des
Batignolles, Courbet coming and going, *The White
Girl,* Jo as Whistler saw her, when compared to
Courbet's *Jo, Femme d'Irlande,* makes it clear that
he was halfway out of Courbet's clutches.

From now on, though different problems absorbed him at different times, he was always himself, a strong, a distinct individuality in his art,
shaped and perfected by the study of tradition,
none the worse for the interval of Realism. Another influence, it is true, was apparent, when he
first broke away from Courbet—the influence of
Japan. He was one of the group—Manet, Fantin,
Baudelaire, the De Goncourts—who learned to
love the Orient in the little shop of Madame Desoye
in the Rue de Rivoli. It was here he first got to
know the blue-and-white, the kakemonos, above
all the color prints and sketch books of China and
Japan. Here he learned that the story of the beau-

tiful is broidered with the birds in the fan of Hokusai even as it is hewn in the marbles of the Parthenon. He never actually adopted Chinese and Japanese methods as he had Courbet's, but the drawings and prints were an inspiration. He loved to have beautiful things about him and he filled his Lindsey Road house with the treasures bought for a song at Madame Desoye's. He clothed Jo in gorgeous garments, placed her in the midst of pots and prints, lacquers and draperies, and painted the *Lange Leizen, The Gold Screen, The Balcony*—as "the Japanese Series" these pictures are usually described. But the most important of them all was the portrait not of Jo but of Miss Spartali, daughter of the Greek Consul in London, a young girl of unusual beauty. Like Jo, she was arrayed for her portrait in Oriental splendor, which well became her rich, exotic beauty, and on canvas she was transformed into *La Princesse du Pays de la Porcelaine.* The marvel is that the painter inspired by this strange beauty could ever have been influenced by that older painter who startled Paris with the matter-of-fact *Bon Jour, Monsieur Courbet.* The Japanese was a passing phase and Whistler worked out of it triumphantly in *The Little White Girl,* a few Japanese details introduced because they happened to be about in the room where Jo posed, but Jo herself no longer masquerading in clothes that did not belong to her, wearing instead her own simple soft

white muslin gown with the puffed sleeves, as she
stands *Before the Mirror,* one arm languidly outstretched on the mantel below it. This was the
painting that inspired Swinburne. He put into
beautiful words the beauty that holds one as a
charm when one chances upon the picture where
it hangs now in the National Gallery.

> *White rose in red rose-garden*
> *Is not so white*

is the impression Jo gives in her soft white muslin,
a vivid Japanese fan in the hand that drops at her
side, rose-tinted azaleas straying against the falling folds of the gown. And with Swinburne one
feels all that is lovely in the face of this "White
rose of weary leaf," in the "bright hair," in the
hand, "a fallen rose," in the "white throat lifted,"
understanding why during long years she was
Whistler's constant model and inseparable companion. It is not strange that Swinburne's tribute
touched Whistler deeply. He was designing his
own frames at the time and he had two verses from
the poem written on the one he chose for *The Little
White Girl.* The pity is that the frame should long
since have disappeared. Such a combination of
painter and poet is rare. Fortunately, Mr. Will Low
possesses a record in an old photograph of the pic-

ture in its original frame, which he allowed us to reproduce in *The Life of Whistler*.

To his study of Japanese art Whistler owed his command of detail, his exquisite dexterity in rendering it, and his critics, who say he omitted detail from his pictures because he could not paint it, have only to be referred to his Japanese series to discover their mistake. Still more important, he also undoubtedly owed to this study, especially of Hiroshige's color prints, the inspiration of his Nocturnes in which, if genius can be said to be more original in one thing than in another, Whistler was most original. He was the first to paint the night. That distinction can be given him without dispute. Here and there, before his time, artists may have attempted to paint things and places seen at night, a few entertained a vague ambition to paint moonlight. But, before Whistler, not one had endeavored to render on canvas the very quality of night, its atmosphere, its color, the depths of its darkness, its mystery, its pale dim light from the stars and the moon; I might almost say no one had ever seen night before. His Nocturnes were scoffed at in the beginning, but now people who are caught in the blue twilight or the paler starlight and condescend to be conscious of the fact, say "How like a Whistler!"

His desire to paint night was stimulated by his knowledge of Hiroshige. This does not mean that

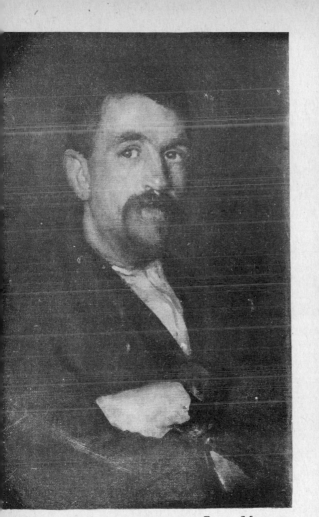

THE MASTER SMITH OF LYME REGIS, *Boston Museum*

he was or wanted to be a copyist, an echo of Hiroshige. The difference in the medium the two men
used would have made such an echo impossible.
Hiroshige, working in flat tints and lines on his
wood-block, suggested night with poetic truth, but
the medium limited him to the suggestion. Whistler, using his brush and paint, could render the
tone, the mystery, the actual truth of night rather
than its symbol. In the earlier Nocturnes he was
haunted by certain details in Japanese design, the
little Butterfly in its panel, or a branch of foliage
straying across the canvas, was often an essential
part of the pattern. If he introduced a bridge into
the composition, as in that perfect Nocturne now
hanging in the Tate Gallery, *Battersea Bridge,* he
placed it on his canvas much as Hiroshige placed
his bridge on his block. But these details, for all
their truth and charm, are not indispensable. The
beauty of night would still fill the canvas if they
were not there and Whistler soon omitted Butterfly
and spray of foliage altogether.

The Nocturnes are simple in effect—a space of
vague blue water under a space of vague blue sky,
buildings on the farther shore, sometimes the
bridge high across the canvas, sometimes a ghostly
sail moving out of the shadows—so that to the
Academically trained public, as to the Judge in
court, there seemed no work in them whatever.
The critics of the day were of the same mind as

Sala who, in our copy of *Thornbury's Legends* which had been his, wrote alongside one of Whistler's delicate illustrations: "clever, sketchy and incomplete, like everything he has done." The Pre-Raphaelites, though in the opposition, had encouraged the belief that the more a painting or drawing revealed the labor of the artist, the more sincere and praiseworthy the achievement. Holman Hunt would boast of the days or weeks he had devoted to one shaving in *The Shadow of the Cross*. But Whistler said, "a picture is finished when all trace to bring about the end has disappeared." The Nocturnes looked simplicity itself, but this simplicity was not achieved without the closest application and industry. He quickly learned that he could not paint night at night. By artificial light he could not see what he was doing, the color that seemed right would in the morning be all wrong. Then he remembered Boisbaudran. He had not studied with Boisbaudran, but Fantin and Legros had, and they probably initiated him in their master's methods. Boisbaudran believed the cultivation of memory indispensable in an artist's training and he would send his students, by day or night, into the streets or the country to visualize what they saw, so exhaustively and so accurately that, back in the studio, they could put it down as accurately on canvas. This was the method Whistler finally adopted for the Nocturnes. Evening after evening he would wander along the Chelsea Embankment, or sit at his window overlooking the Thames in Lindsey Row, and study the river and the Battersea shore and the sky and the passing boats until he had the whole picture by heart. Usually some one was with him to whom, after he had mastered his lesson, he would repeat it, recalling the arrangement of color and line and every detail. If he made any mistake in his recitation he would turn to his study again and yet again until his description was faultless. After this he would go to bed, absorbed in the subject and immediately in the morning begin to put it on canvas with the large brushes and the very liquid paint he prepared for the purpose. If all went well, the Nocturne was finished, as he told the Judge in court, in a couple of days.

Night is rarely so beautiful, so mysterious anywhere as in London, and his windows and the Embankment were never exhausted. But sometimes he wandered on down to Westminster, sometimes to Cremorne Gardens which gave him *The Falling Rocket*—the coxcomb's paint pot—or he left London for Southampton perhaps, or went as far as Valparaiso, bringing back two of the loveliest of the series. The upright *Valparaiso Bay—Blue and Gold* was the first Nocturne he exhibited, though it may not have been the first he painted. In the beginning he called these pictures *Moonlights*.

When he changed this to *Nocturnes,* critics and public were outraged as they would most likely not have been had they known that the title originated not with Whistler but with Leyland. When Leyland suggested it, Whistler was enchanted:

"I can't thank you too much for the name Nocturne as the title for my Moonlights. You have no idea what an irritation it proves to the critics and consequent pleasure to me; besides it is really so charming, and does so practically say all I want to say and *no more* than I wish."

In his portraits as well, Whistler was escaping from the last touch of Japanese influence and Courbet's. As his knowledge of beauty increased he learned these two facts—realism is not the solution of the problem of art, color will yield as perfect a design as detail. "As music is the poetry of sound," he wrote, "so is painting the poetry of sight, and the subject matter has nothing to do with harmony of sound or of color," which was Greek and Latin to the public of his day. Popular painters racked their brains and every available book of reference for a story or an allegory or an historic event to paint and, when they found what they sought, they shut themselves up in their studios for fear a less fortunate rival might steal it. "Art should be independent of all clap-trap—should stand alone, and appeal to the artistic sense of eye or ear, without confounding this with emo-

PORTRAIT OF HIS MOTHER, *The Louvre*

tions entirely foreign to it, as devotion, pity, love, patriotism, and the like. All these have no kind of concern with it and that is why I insist on calling my works 'arrangements' and 'harmonics':" a little paragraph which is the keynote to the ends and aims of his life as artist. And the irony of it is that Whistler, a shameless Pagan to the patrons of the "painted photograph" and the story-telling picture, has become to modern authorities a Puritan because he concentrated interest on the least human and the least living elements in a work of art.

In the long series of portraits, beginning with the *Mother* and *Carlyle*, the experiments of the student are at an end, the knowledge of the master triumphs. He let there be no mistake about the aims he now set himself. His portraits were *Arrangements* in color, *Symphonies*, *Harmonies*, *Variations*. Again the critics raved. When the *Mother—Arrangement in Gray and Black, No. 1*, was succeeded by *Thomas Carlyle, Arrangement in Gray and Black, No. 2*, they deplored his limited palette and limited stock of ideas. For both portraits he chose not merely the same title but the same gray wall with the same frames hanging on it, the same black dado; in both the figure was seen in profile seated on a cane-bottomed chair against this wall. True, the curtain in the portrait of his Mother does not reappear in the portrait of Carlyle; the details of costume are necessarily different, though not the color. Of the difference in the character of the two sitters—the Mother serene and placid, Carlyle weary and impatient—of Whistler's profound appreciation of this difference, the critics could see nothing. Nor could they appreciate the appropriateness of the same composition and color scheme for two old people with whom age had had its way.

Carlyle looks so conscious of his martyrdom as sitter that it is a comfort to know that something in the portrait pleased him. Watts had painted him not long before and, after much of what Carlyle called "meestification," showed him the portrait and asked how he liked it. He looked at it. "Mon, I would have ye know I am in the hobit of wurin' clean lunnen," was his one comment. He was satisfied with the "lunnen" Whistler supplied, and they got on well together though at the start it seemed as if there would be trouble. When Carlyle came for the first sitting he sat down and said, "Now, mon, fire away!" Whistler's face must have shown that that wasn't how he worked, for Carlyle quickly added, "If ye're fighting battles or painting pictures, the only thing to do is to fire away."

The *Carlyle* was not finished when Whistler began his *Miss Alexander*. It is said that the old man and the little girl met at the door one day and that when Carlyle heard she had come for a sit-

ting, he shook his head and murmured "Puir
lassie! Puir lassie!" A touch of sullenness in the
expression of her face in the portrait suggests that
she was of the same way of thinking, as well she
might for Whistler required no less than seventy
sittings before he had done. This portrait is proof
positive that lack of imagination was not responsible for his painting two *Arrangements in Black
and Gray* in succession. His imagination was in
divining character and inventing the terms of
color in which it could be best expressed. He could
discriminate between old age and childhood, and
for little Miss Alexander the *Harmony* was in
Gray and Green. He superintended every detail of
the dress in talks and correspondence with Mrs.
Alexander, going into careful explanation as to the
quality and the laundering of the muslin gown,
the manner of rosette worn at the waist, the droop
of feather and hat held in the little hand. In this
portrait of childhood he let butterflies flutter above
the child's head and daisies blossom on canvas at
her side. And the little English girl is as lovely as
the Louvre's little Infanta by Velasquez.

The *Miss Alexander* did not exhaust Whistler's
imagination or his resources. Almost all his large
full-length portraits belong to those two agitated,
agitating decades, the Seventies and Eighties, and
for each portrait the design is as original as the
study of character is penetrating—Mrs. Huth in

severe black velvet and old lace, and Mrs. Leyland
in soft rose-flushed muslin, a branch of rose-flushed
almond blossom carrying out the Harmony; Leyland, "the Liverpool Medici," in frilled shirt and
buckled shoes, and Irving, a third *Arrangement
in Black* but the black relieved by notes and pas-
sages of silver gray; stately Rosa Corder and Maud
—Jo's successor—her face like a delicate flower in
The Fur Jacket; Lady Archibald Campbell, slim,
aristocratic, and Lady Meux, buxom, of the people;
—and these do not complete the list of the portraits
done in the difficult years of the lawsuit, the bankruptcy, the struggle with debt, by the artist re-
proached for doing so little.

In all, save the Mrs. Leyland, he dispensed with
superfluous accessories, depending for effect on
pose, on line, on color, on atmosphere, on the principles he had put into words with surprisingly
clear brevity. His canvases justified his *Propositions.* His work does not reek of the sweat of his
brow, his men and women, as he painted them, do
stand upon their legs and well within the frame.
This last was to him of supreme importance.

"The frame is, indeed, the window through
which the painter looks at his model, and nothing
could be more offensively inartistic than the brutal
attempt to thrust the model on the hitherside of this
window."

And he thought that if in a gallery, with the

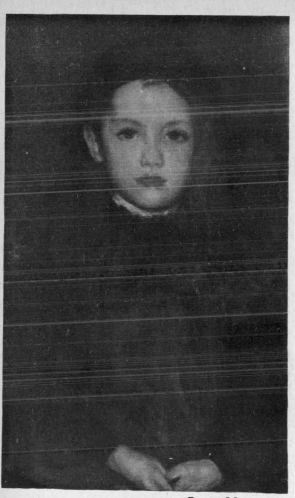

LITTLE ROSE OF LYME REGIS, *Boston Museum*

power of comparison it provided, "the people" would look upon their passing fellow creatures they might perceive, if dimly, "how little they resemble the impudent images on the walls! how 'quiet' in color they are! how 'gray' how 'low in tone!' And then it might be explained to their riveted intelligence how they had mistaken mere-triciousness for mastery, and by what mean methods the imposture had been practiced upon them." But the people did not look, nor did the critics except to seek that which Whistler never meant them to find. They were mostly like George Moore, who was concerned with the big things Whistler might have done had he had the physical strength to tackle them. It would be as wise to criticize Vermeer because he never painted Anatomy Lessons and Regent Pictures.

After the Eighties Whistler finished compara-tively few large full-length portraits. Early in the Nineties he was distracted by the move back to Paris, by his preparation for the Retrospective Ex-hibition at Goupil's in London, which marked the turning of the tide in his favor, and, almost im-mediately afterwards, by the illness and death of his wife. He was devoted to her, he was never quite the same after she had gone, and the last few years of the Nineties he was himself fighting against death. Two portraits of Mrs. Charles Whibley— *Andalouse* and *La Tulipe,* a full-length of himself

which was destroyed, a George Vanderbilt, fine a
one stage but painted out and over to its ruin as
last saw it, Miss Kinsella that fared little better—
these were virtually all the large portraits of note
The portraits were usually half-lengths, just th
head and shoulders, none finer than *The Maste
Smith of Lyme Regis* and *Little Rose,* both now i
the Boston Museum of Fine Arts. His increasin
physical weakness did not weaken his faith in th
principles he had laid down for himself, nor hi
adherence to them in his performance. There wa
no falling off. I often heard him say that in th
master's work there could be no better, no worse
Art knows no such distinction.

To these last years belong the beautiful littl
seas painted at Pourville and Dieppe, and one o
two at Domburg. They are small in size, as ar
almost all his paintings of that period. He had no
the vigor left to attack large canvases. But the
are as masterly as the Nocturnes, quiet seas as ;
rule, the movement in the long swell of the waves
in a few the water is ruffled and breaks with whit
foam as *The Freshening Breeze* blows over it. Bu
whether the sea was quiet or troubled, in the small
est canvas he gave it all its bigness.

Unlike many painters, he made no secret of hi
methods. "The secret is in doing it," he maintained
and you have only to study those small marines, hi
water-colors and pastels, to know that his was ;

ecret too profound and personal to be shared. The
ittle pastels he made in Venice are slight simple
ketches in black chalk on brown paper, here and
here a touch of color. But try to make one like
hem. Only the other day an artist said to me,
"They seem so simple," but look into them, attempt
o use his method and you discover fast enough
heir wonderful subtlety. Borrow, as you hope,
hose little touches of color and your difficulties
egin.

I am told that Whistler is out of date in the
tudios to-day. The younger men have no use for
him, which is natural, for the younger men do not
elieve in technical training—the idea that an
rtist should start by mastering his trade is sadly
ld-fashioned. But if these younger men would
pare the time to look attentively into his work,
hey might discover its subtlety, the art with which
ts simplicity is attained, and, though they might
hrink from endeavoring to gain his knowledge at
he cost of the endless training it implies, at least
heir respect for Whistler might be increased.

V

WHISTLER THE ARTIST: HIS PRINTS

WHEN Whistler recalled his early years, it was over the West Point period he sentimentalized. Time glorified the Military Academy in his eyes. It became his standard of conduct. As a West Point man he knew just what to do on every occasion, just how to face friend and foe. In the copy of his *Art and Art Critics* which he sent to the Library he wrote, "From an old cadet whose pride it is to remember his West Point days." He could not talk of West Point without revealing depths of sentiment of which few suspected him.

To the months in the Coast Survey, however, he owed far more practically than to the years at West Point. But memories of his clerkship were not tinged with sentiment. To be a clerk in a Government office was to tumble into the matter-of-fact after having swaggered as an officer in the United States Army. And yet, it was Whistler the clerk who obtained the thorough training in the technique of etching that enabled Whistler the student to produce masterpieces of the art of etching. It taught him no more than West Point had taught

PORTRAIT OF WHISTLER

him of the art of drawing. But it equipped him
technically as an etcher. Those who had never heard
of his early experience in Washington often marveled how he acquired such complete technical
skill so early in his career. Etching in the Eighteen-
Fifties had not drifted into the popularity it suffers
to-day when students and artists, untrained and
unfitted, turn to it as an easy means of making
money. It was mostly in the hands of amateurs—
Seymour Haden in London, the De Goncourts in
Paris. Meryon is the one professional name of importance that stands out, though there are plates
to the credit of Jacque and Millet and others. The
student who wanted to etch, and he was the rare
exception, must have had difficulty in finding a
master. And here was this young American, without art training, who knew all about grounding
and biting his plate and whose command of the
medium enabled him to draw on copper as freely
as on paper, in a restaurant or the studio of a friend,
on a summer holiday with one of the most confirmed *flâneurs* who ever lived, or in the sedate
family circle of his sister's house in London.

It was just because he could use etching in this
fashion that it attracted him in the beginning. The
copper plate is more appropriate for a sketch, for
the record of an impression than canvas and has
the further value of being easier to carry about.
Moreover it was to him a most sympathetic

medium, as sympathetic as paint. He was a born etcher, as Rembrandt was. Without the Coast Survey training he would have etched, but then he could not have begun at once. He would have had to learn how. As it was, he had learned in the best school—a technical school. He had little to unlearn, as, to his regret, he had much, or thought he had, in painting.

After less than four years in Paris, *The French Set—Douze Eaux-Fortes d'après Nature*—was published and already in the prints of this series he is far more personal than in his early paintings, far more distinctly original. It is possible to detect the Louvre and Courbet in his first work as painter, but in *Saverne,* that precursor of his Nocturnes, *The Unsafe Tenement, La Marchande de Moutarde,* it is impossible to point to any one save Whistler—the serious Whistler whom even Paris was long in discovering. He no doubt had seen Rembrandt's etchings and appreciated them and learned something from them, but already in his first prints the line is Whistler's if reminiscent here and there of West Point and the Coast Survey. The way of looking at the subject is Whistler's, the design is Whistler's. Of the gay Whistler, the only Whistler according to his fellow British students, there is not a hint, not a suggestion, except in the title to the *Set* where he himself figures in the big hat Paris and London were never tired of talking about—the big hat of low crown and wide brim, straw because it is summer,—sitting on a sketching stool, his plate supported against his knees, a group of children gathered round him, staring with that steady half-witted stare that drives less seasoned artists back into their studios. Whistler seems imperturbable, but then the tradition is that it is not Whistler who sits there, but Ernest Delannoy who put on the big hat, crouched on the stool, drew up his knees for an easel, endured the staring children, and posed as Whistler for Whistler.

For these French plates Delâtre did most of the printing, and he taught Whistler a great deal about printing which was not, could not be taught at the Coast Survey office. Art is not the special concern of printers of official plates. When he was in London doing *The Thames Set*, as I have said, Serjeant Thomas and his son Ralph had Delâtre over from Paris to print this Series as well, with Whistler, and it was really not until the Venice period that Whistler undertook almost all his own printing himself.

In London Whistler, at work out of doors, did not mind the burden of copper plates any more than he had in Paris or on the tramp with Ernest. He fell in love at first sight with the Thames, the commercial Thames flowing through London, looked down upon as unacademic by superior English critics and artists. When he wanted to paint any of the inexhaustible subjects it supplied, he was apt to stay in the old Cherry Gardens inn with the bulging windows and balconies over the river, or else at home after he had a home on the river bank. But to get to know the Thames as he determined to know it, it was best to wander, along the wharves, on the docks, on the low mud banks, and during his wanderings it was simpler to carry copper plates for his impressions of the picturesqueness which was ever-changing and to-morrow might not be as to-day. There were long wanderings, from *Millbank* to *Black Lion Wharf*, *Limehouse*, *Billingsgate*, *Rotherhithe*, to the busy haunts ignored by fastidious Londoners and immortalized by Whistler. He saw the Thames, as he saw night, that is, as nobody else had ever seen it before, and all he saw—its shipping, its warehouses, its little inns, its movement, its dock hands, its curious riverside types—he drew with a minuteness, a feeling for character, a truth, a care, disturbing to the authorities who had dismissed him contemptuously and had so often said he could not draw that everybody believed it. Everybody in the Sixties would have considered it another rare jest could they have foreseen Rodin's beautiful tribute: "Whistler's art will lose nothing by the lapse of time; it will gain; for one of its qualities is energy, another is delicacy; but the greatest of all is its mastery of drawing." The mastery is already in these Thames plates, with their beautiful render-

THE KITCHEN

ing of detail, their careful observation, their sympathetic study. The elaborate working out of detail was good discipline from which he gained his later freedom, his later knowledge of what to leave out as well as what to put in.

Hanging on our walls in our Buckingham Street chambers was Whistler's *Adam and Eve—Old Chelsea*, to which Joseph Pennell would point as the connecting link between the elaboration of detail in the Thames etchings and the suggestiveness of the Venice etchings. In the *Adam and Eve* much of the detail is given but it is suggested rather than elaborately drawn. In the Venice Series it is almost altogether suggested. He gave scarcely any outline. He depended more and more for his effects on different bitings and on the printing. As in London, his wanderings in Venice were journeys of discovery. He followed no man's trail but blazed a new one for himself. It led him to his *Traghetto* and *Riva*, *Rialto* and *Nocturne—Palaces*, *Lagoon* and *Bridge*, to so many more subjects than the commissioned twelve could include that a second *Set*, of twenty-six,—though not all of Venice— was issued within a year or two. As he etched now, he had to do his own printing. And he had learned from experience that, as Joseph Pennell wrote in *The Adventures of an Illustrator*: "All artists who really etch pull their own proofs, for the printing of a plate is as vital to its success as drawing or biting." No professional printer could have got what he did and what he wanted out of his plates. And to print on that historic old Venice press was the hardest of hard labor and dangerous as well, for sometimes the bed would fall out. One had to be on one's guard. He went on with the printing when he got back to London, chiefly in two rooms the Fine Art Society rented for him in Air Street, within convenient distance of the Gallery. His was a new method of working on copper—a more painter-like method than ever had been attempted before—and when the prints were exhibited, they increased the discomfort of the critics, who were fearful lest in pronouncing judgment they might convict themselves. Those who were least afraid ventured to be honest and say boldly what most thought, that here was another crop of Whistler's little jokes.

Is it any wonder that Whistler was embittered? In Venice he had worked at a pace with which few other artists could keep up. Before the world in London he was the gay trifler, with the long cane and the ribbon-led Pomeranian dog, but shut away from the world he was toiling as hard as a day laborer and without a Labor Union's limit to the hours of his day. The plates that came of the toiling in Venice and London were masterpieces, they stand alone in the history of etching. Having no doubt himself of the greatness of his accomplish-

nent, what could he feel save bitterness when the
public jeered and joked and treated him as a
mountebank who, for its amusement, was doing his
turn on copper?

Few *Sets* were sold in London. Ernest Brown of
the Fine Arts Society brought them to New York.
Eight *Sets* were ordered, that was all. And to-day
none but the millionaire or the speculating dealer
can afford to buy them when they are up for sale
in the auction rooms.

Wherever Whistler might go, etching plates and
etching needle went with him—that delicate, excellently balanced little needle made for Whistler
by a surgical instrument maker in Paris, now
copied, but clumsily, and commercially known as
the Whistler Needle. There were many more London etchings. He never was in Venice again, but
occasionally he would wander in Belgium, in Holland, in France, and plates and needle were not
left behind. When, as President of the British
Artists, he attended the Naval Review at the time
of Queen Victoria's Jubilee, he had with him as
usual, a number of small plates and his needle, and
the fine Series of the twelve etchings done in the
one day are the artistic record of that event. To
work out-of-doors is something of an ordeal no
matter where you may be. Begin to paint or draw
or etch in the street and the crowd gathers with
the same inane curiosity that draws it irresistibly to

the spectacle of men digging a hole or laying a gas-
pipe. From my journeys with Joseph Pennell I
should say that nowhere can people be so offensive
to artists as in Holland, the home of art. Whistler
did not escape when he was there. In the Canals of
Amsterdam he worked from a boat. Once a woman
at a window of the high houses emptied buckets
of filthy water over him, and he had to call the
police. After that once, he said, he had no further
trouble, because a policeman always came along
with him in the boat. In Brussels, in the Grande
Place, he was hemmed in by the curious but they
were more easily scattered. He had only to point
at them with his sharp needle and to shriek the
"Ha! ha!" so effective in London, and they fled.
Nothing daunted Whistler when it was a question
of work.

And this Idle Apprentice could never be idle.
If he was not etching in the street or painting in
the studio, he was drawing, jotting down notes
on paper. If a chance pose of his model or a sitter
pleased him, in the intervals of rest, out came paper,
pencil, chalk or pastels. For a while in the Sixties
he never went to bed without making a drawing
of himself. Sitting with us in the evening after
dinner he would sketch with a handy pen or pencil
on a bit of paper, hardly conscious of what he was
doing, the beautiful nude of his last pastel or the
figure in the painting he had been working on all

ANNIE HADEN, IN THE BIG HAT

day. He preferred to etch when he could because of his great love for the medium, a love shared by all genuine etchers. Besides, it is hard to say why, though it is not strange, the artist is rare who has not pleasure in multiplying his work. He who creates is too generous to wish to keep his creations for himself alone. The poet is not satisfied until he has published his poems. When the artist makes his drawing on paper, there is one drawing and that is all. But when he etches a plate it will give him twenty-five, fifty, sometimes a hundred good prints. After Whistler had been etching for some years he was introduced to a medium that could multiply still more autographically and still more abundantly than etching. This medium was lithography. In etching the biting, a chemical process, comes between the artist's original drawing and the printed result. Lithography gives the artist his actual drawing unchanged by any process. Lithography is the multiplication of the original drawing, etching is the multiplication of the etched drawing—there is a difference.

Thomas Way, the commercial lithographic printer, was the first to draw Whistler's attention to lithography and help him to understand what it can really do. In the Seventies, when Way approached Whistler on the subject, artistic lithography was and had been long under a cloud. Commerce had appropriated and made a hateful thing

of it and given it a bad name. Few remembered the
work of the great lithographers in the great days
of the art—Géricault and Delacroix, Charlet and
Raffet, Daumier and Gavarni, Goya and Menzel.
One of its great advantages was considered a great
drawback. The stone could yield an almost unlim-
ited edition, therefore the dealer's game of strictly
limited editions could not be so readily played with
lithography as with etching. However, Whistler's
one interest was to find out what the stone and
lithographic chalk and lithographic washes and
lithographic stump would give him. With what
they gave he was enchanted. To the surprise of the
Ways his lithographs were perfect from the beginning. But Thomas Way had come to him in his
most troubled period, the period of the Peacock
Room, the Ruskin Trial, the Bankruptcy. After
these first experiments he was off to Venice where
his immediate business was to etch. The Eighties
were for him as troubled as the Seventies, though
in another fashion. It was not until the last decade
of the last century that he continued his experiments, devoted more time to them, became absorbed in lithography as he had hitherto been in
etching. He did not give up etching but he quickly
realized that often when he was not prepared to
etch, it was possible to make lithographs.

His wife died in 1896 after her long, heart-
rending illness. During the two or three years of

this illness, for her sake they traveled from town
to town and, in London, moved from hotel to
hotel. Sometimes he was without a studio, sometimes he worked in studios lent by friends. Condi-
tions were uncertain at the best, interruptions
were incessant. It seemed almost as if lithography
was invented to rescue him from despair during
these miserable years. When he had a studio he
painted. When he was without a studio, etching
presented difficulties. Copper plates are heavy, hotel
sitting rooms are hardly convenient or appropriate
for acid baths. To make his lithographs he needed
simply small sheets of transfer paper and a lithographic pencil or two. He had given up stone almost at the beginning. Stones are heavier than copper plates and Way's men were not always at hand
to lug them about for him. He had a little sort of
case or portfolio made for his sheets of transfer
paper—his lithographs were always small—and
once his drawing was finished, all he had to do was
to take or send it to the Ways who transferred
it to the stone and printed it, and he never allowed
them to print many. He limited his editions.

It chanced that at the same period, lithography
was approaching the centenary of its invention.
Diligent efforts were made to revive it, not so en-
thusiastically in London as in Paris, and artists
know, or should know, what fine work came of the
effort. Whistler had anticipated the movement, was

in no way influenced by this, unfortunately, passing mode in the studios. He would have persevered in making his lithographs had he been the one artist to touch stone or transfer paper, had no collector or dealer shown an interest in them. It was the medium of all others that provided him with unfailing resources during the most grievous troubles that he, the man of many troubles, had to live through. The little case in his pocket was always ready and, absorbed in work, his sadness was relieved at least for an interval.

His many different subjects explain how often he turned to it for relief. On his transfer paper he drew the little shops and gardens of Paris, the streets and smithies of Lyme Regis, the churches and the Thames of London, and indoors there were friends to pose for him. A sad Whistler he had become, almost unrecognizable to those who could not imagine any but the gay Whistler. Towards the end he stayed at the Savoy in London, where the beauty of the Thames he loved was just out of his windows. He was but a five minutes' walk from our Buckingham Street chambers and often, late in the afternoon, he would drop in, for his sadness only increased his unwillingness to stay alone. During those afternoons he made the quite wonderful series of portraits of Joseph Pennell and the one portrait of myself. I think he felt that this one was enough. I certainly did. I appreciated the

BLACK LION WHARF

honor of sitting for Whistler, but I did not appreciate the appearance I present in his lithograph. Nor did he. He had only six prints pulled and on the one he sent me he wrote "With sincere apologies," which I honestly believe I deserved.

His lithographs are delicate, gray, silvery impressions of the things and people that interested him and seemed appropriate to the medium. They are full of character in the rendering of the subject, but with little variety in the method used and the effects obtained, though lithography allows of inexhaustible variety. The reason is that Whistler never knew anything about lithography beyond drawing on the transfer paper or the stone. Of transferring and printing, he remained in complete ignorance. Much mystery then hung about the lithographer's shop. Whistler, I believe, never penetrated as far as the printing presses, never saw his drawing transferred or printed. The marvel is that, under these circumstances, his lithographs are masterpieces. And yet, remembering the technical variety in his etchings, one sighs for the things he might have done had he been his own printer, had he ever been allowed to work with his printer.

VI

WHISTLER THE ARTIST: HIS WRITING

WHATEVER Whistler undertook to do he succeeded in doing astonishingly well. When he began to write his pamphlets and *Propositions* and letters to the press it was with the finish and distinction of a practiced writer. This was partly because always that which his hand found to do he did with all his might, partly because he was the artist who could not be satisfied with the crude, the slipshod or the commonplace.

People who could appreciate good writing asked with amazement how he had managed to develop his style. Unquestionably Mrs. Whistler's stern Biblical discipline was in a large measure responsible. From the daily morning recital of the Psalms and other texts he acquired a knowledge of the Scriptures that was of immense service to him throughout life. It equipped him from his youth with a high literary standard, familiarity with good English, and a useful supply of appropriate quotations. What it meant to him from a religious standpoint I would not venture to say. That he cherished some sort of belief in another world, in a

hereafter, I gathered from the way he scoffed when
I admitted my skepticism. That his faith in the
other world was strong enough for him to believe
also in the possibility of communicating with it,
I know for a fact from the stories he told me of
the wonderful evenings he and Jo spent with
planchette, the forerunner of the present ouija
board. Another point of view was explained by
his description of the Bible as "that splendid mine
of invective." But what he actually thought of it,
what manner of Christian it made of him, how far
it inspired him in his attitude towards life, is another matter. He seldom talked of religion. The
one thing certain is that it had a tremendous influence on his writing, and there remains *The Gentle Art of Making Enemies* as proof.

If my knowledge of the Bible was as intimate
as his, I could no doubt trace to the source in book
and text many a turn of a sentence, many an illu-
sion in pamphlets and letters. But I was brought up
in the Church that does not give the Scriptures for
daily food to babes and sucklings, and I am positive only when I come upon something as obvious
as "the crackling of thorns under a pot" or "the
many mansions in my father's House," upon char-
acters as familiar to everybody as Balaam's ass, or
ce coquin d'Habacuc. His quotations and references
of the kind are numerous but anybody can quote
from the Bible, and unfortunately too many do

without understanding or discrimination. Its influence on Whistler was far greater, went far deeper. His mother was concerned with his soul alone when she based his early training on the Bible. She could not have imagined, nor would she have cared, that thanks to this training he never in literature had to lament the things to be unlearned. He knew the best from the start. King James' version was his standard, his style was derived from it. With such a standard he could not go wrong, though he might be writing nothing more serious than a challenge to "Oscar" for a duel of wit or a dismissal of "Arry"—Harry Quilter—destined to be rescued from the Great Silence by Whistler's ridicule.

In that first pamphlet, *Art and Art Critics,* there was no trace of the amateur. It had point, it had vigor, it had humor, it abounded in gay relentless cruelty to "the enemies." The balance in statement and argument was as perfect as the color in his Harmonies, the line in his etchings. He wished an unbiased report of his lawsuit to go down to posterity and he knew that he was the one of all others to prepare it. He was not writing in his own defense nor as a defender of Art, which needs none. His object was to expose the empty pretensions of the critics who would take Art under their protection and play the guide to artists. He might not have written at all had it not been for Ruskin's

WEARY

attack. But he used Ruskin simply as a type, a representative of the whole tribe of art critics who, in their ignorance, would make and unmake the reputation of artists with a public as ignorant. The tribe has not disappeared; in their self-sufficiency, they continue to pose as patrons and authorities, though with less reason than Ruskin, who had studied the rudiments of art and could draw with delicacy and charm. Whistler's summing up is a fine example of the force, directness and rhythm of his prose:

"Still, quite alone, stands Ruskin, whose writing is art, and whose art is unworthy his writing. To him and his example do we owe the outrage of proffered assistance from the unscientific—the meddling of the immodest—the intrusion of the garrulous. Art, that for ages has hewn its own history in marble, and written its own comments on canvas, shall it suddenly stand still, and stammer, and wait for wisdom from the passer-by?—for guidance from the hand that holds neither brush nor chisel? Out upon the shallow conceit! What greater sarcasm can Mr. Ruskin pass upon himself than that he preaches to young men what he cannot perform! Why, unsatisfied with his own conscious power, should he choose to become the type of incompetence by talking for forty years of what he has never done!

"Let him resign his present professorship, to fill

the Chair of Ethics at the University. As master of English literature, he has a right to his laurels, while, as the popularizer of pictures he remains the Peter Parley of painting."

I have often thought, as did Joseph Pennell, that had Whistler seen Ruskin's drawings he might not have swept Ruskin's right to criticize so ruthlessly away. Certainly, he granted Ruskin his literary laurels graciously enough. He was ever the first to recognize and extol good work in any medium. He would not have had much sympathy with Ruskin's method of drawing but he would have admitted its honesty. However that may be, this passage is as complete and powerful and unanswerable a denunciation of the art critic who is not an artist as was ever written, true to-day as it was yesterday, as it will be to-morrow.

Had this been Whistler's sole publication all I have said of him as writer would call for no modification. It may be that he sprinkled French words and quotations overliberally. That he should sprinkle them was natural, inevitable. He spoke French as well as English and to many of the delicate little things he wished to say, delicate little stabs he wished to give, French is more eloquently adapted, and to that end he used it often and with unfailing effect. But in *Art and Art Critics* the sprinkling is almost overdone. The pamphlet also loses by comparison with his *Ten O'Clock*, but ten

years separate the two and he had had frequent
practice in the meantime—letters to the papers,
one series issued as *The Piker Papers,* and the first
set of *Propositions.* Practice hardly accounts for the
perfection of style he had developed when he made
his profession of faith, first from the lecture platform and then in print. Read *Ten O'Clock* for
this profession, the artist's creed; read it again for
sheer pleasure in the beauty of the written word.
Quotation does it scant justice but, as a reminder
of its rare quality, I must quote once more the
often quoted passage in which Whistler is supreme
as artist and writer:

"And when the evening mist clothes the riverside
with poetry, as with a veil, and the poor buildings
lose themselves in the dim sky, and the tall chimneys become campanili, and the warehouses are
palaces in the night, and the whole city hangs in
the heavens, and fairyland is before us—then the
wayfarer hastens home; the workingman and the
cultured one, the wise man and the one of pleasure, cease to understand, as they have ceased to
see, and Nature, who, for once, has sung in tune,
sings her exquisite song to the artist alone, her son
and her master—her son in that he loves her, her
master in that he knows her."

Whistler had no patience with "genius work."
He worked hard to reach perfection in his paintings and prints, and so he worked hard to reach

perfection in his writing. As he got the subject by heart before he painted his Nocturnes, so he got his *Ten O'Clock* by heart before he carried it to the platform. Again he went through a fever of study, of recitation to his friends, of inventing and correcting. Much talk of the *"mot juste"* was current in the Nineties and is now among the present chroniclers at second-hand of that decade. But by none of the great little men of the Nineties was the "right word" so carefully considered, so weighed in the balance, as by Whistler in the Eighties. The King James' translators of the Scriptures had found it always and so would he, at the price of no matter how many struggles, no matter what agony of spirit. He would descend upon one friend at dinner to read him a new page, he would rouse another at midnight to submit a new paragraph. About his theme he never had a moment's doubt or hesitation. London was living in a fool's paradise of art where every duffer, who dabbled with paint or acid and could write R.A. after his name, was a born genius. It was the great period of the Academy, therefore a great art period, even as the Age of Pericles in Greece, the Age of the Renaissance in Italy. Whistler shattered this comfortable confidence in Academic infallibility. There was no artistic period, never an art-loving nation—art happens, he proclaimed, a disconcerting truth to the faithful who thronged the Burlington House Exhibitions, as it

would be to-day when efforts at self-expression
fill the galleries with masterpieces and America
alone produces "fifty best etchings" in a year. For
the benefit of the unbelievers he sketched rapidly,
brilliantly the history of Art's happening, from
the beginning when men went forth each day to
battle, to hunt, to dig, but one among them "dif-
fering from the rest . . . stayed by the tents with the
women, and traced strange devices with a burnt
stick upon a 'gourd' ";
until

". . . the sunny morning, when, with her glorious
Greek relenting, she [Art] yielded up the secret of
repeated line, as, with his hand in hers, together
they marked in marble, the measured rhyme of
lovely limb and draperies flowing in unison, to the
day, when she dipped the Spaniard's brush in light
and air . . . ages had gone by and few had been
her choice.

·   ·   ·   ·   ·   ·

"We have then but to wait—until, with the mark
of the Gods upon him—there come among us again
the chosen—who shall continue what has gone before. Satisfied that, even were he never to appear,
the story of the beautiful is already complete—
hewn in the marbles of the Parthenon—and broidered, with the birds, upon the fan of Hokusai—
at the foot of Fusiyama."

Probably no audience was ever so puzzled as

Whistler's at Prince's Hall in London on the evening of February 20, 1885. The name of the lecture startled them—was it deliberate eccentricity?—though Whistler meant nothing more startling than to name an hour which would allow people the luxury of finishing their dinner to the last drop of coffee and the last cigarette, without haste and yet arrive in time for their arrival not to be a nuisance to him. They were more puzzled by his seriousness—sure that the sardonic "Ha! ha!" must suddenly echo through that polite meeting place, transform it into a circus, and turn them into ridicule for coming, for being there. Newspaper men decided to be on the safe side and, as if the "Ha! ha!" was really ringing in their ears, reported the general feeling of the audience to be wonder as to whether "the eccentric artist was going to sketch, to pose, to sing or to rhapsodize," and then astonishment that the "amiable eccentric appeared as a jaunty, unabashed, composed and self-satisfied gentleman, armed with an opera hat and an eyeglass." Oscar Wilde was afraid not to hedge and he carried off the hedging with alliteration, describing Whistler as "a miniature Mephistopheles mocking the majority." An exception here and there in the audience may have realized the privilege of listening to the most sincere and beautiful profession of faith ever made by an artist to an unworthy public. But the many sneered or laughed, for to them Whistler was still the mountebank.

It was the serious Whistler, who wrote *Ten O'Clock*. Art was the subject, on his part there was no jesting, and it is worth noting that that evening in Prince's Hall his earnestness produced a sort of stage-fright, the only time he was ever accused of shyness.

The gay, joyous Whistler dealt afterwards with the critics, their stupidity a goad to his wit. Oscar Wilde was the scapegoat, Oscar who in the Eighties posed flamboyantly as the infallible Apostle of Art, the one and only wit of the day. Whistler did not spare him. Oscar was offensive in *The Pall Mall Gazette*. Whistler laughed lightly in *The World*:

". . . what has Oscar in common with Art? except that he dines at our tables and picks from our platters the plums for the pudding he peddles in the provinces. Oscar—the amiable, irresponsible, esurient Oscar—with no more sense of a picture than of the fit of a coat, has the courage of the opinions . . . of others!"

The next week in the same paper came Oscar's thrust:

"Atlas, this is very sad! With our James vulgarity begins at home and should be allowed to stay there."

Another week, and then the joyful laugh from Whistler:

"A poor thing, Oscar! but for once, I suppose your own."

Edmund Yates, the editor of *The World,* signed himself Atlas and was addressed as Atlas by his correspondents whom, if as prominent as Whistler or Oscar Wilde, he encouraged. He delighted in Whistler's wit and agility in an argument, and would sometimes spur him on when he had been overlong silent, always ready to print what he wrote, to make the Butterfly a "feature." The correspondence is in *The Gentle Art,* the book in which Whistler gathered together as much of his correspondence as he wished to preserve, and dedicated "To the Rare Few, who, early in Life, have rid themselves of the Friendship of the Many." He and Yates understood each other and, if they did not always agree, met the situation with a sense of the fun in their disagreeing. Atlas once published a letter from Whistler to Oscar Wilde, in it a reference to Sidney Colvin, Slade Professor, and with a sudden access of politeness or caution printed not his full name, but his initials. In another editor Whistler might have resented this tampering. But to Atlas he wrote—and Atlas published it:

". . . How unlike me! Instead of the frank reck-lessness which has unfortunately become a characteristic, I am, for the first time, disguised in careful timidity, and discharge my insinuating initials from the ambush of innuendo.

ADAM AND EVE—OLD CHELSEA

"My dear Atlas, if I may not always call a spade a spade, may I not call a Slade Professor Sidney Colvin?"

Below the Butterfly writhes uproariously, its tail curling with well-aimed sting in mocking glee. And you turn one page and you find the first *Propositions* Whistler issued. The Butterfly draws in its sting and Whistler is seriousness itself. This contrast throughout the book between the two Whistlers lends the value of biography to *The Gentle Art*.

At intervals two other sets of *Propositions* appeared and all three are difficult to quote from because, in each, one clause depends so entirely upon another. Etching is the subject of the first and the argument is to prove "that in Art it is criminal to go beyond the means used in its exercise," which explains why, to Whistler, the large plate was an "offense," the triumph of the "duffer." In *Propositions—No. 2* the truth established is that "a picture is finished when all trace of the means used to bring about the end has disappeared." For, is the conclusion:

"The masterpiece should appear as the flower to the painter—perfect in its bud as in its bloom—with no reason to explain its presence—no mission to fulfill—a joy to the artist—a delusion to the philanthropist—a puzzle to the botanist—an accident of sentiment and alliteration to the literary man."

To *A Further Proposition* I have already referred. Its theme is the treatment of flesh and the mistake of the "unsuspecting painter in making his man stand out from the frame." "The Master from Madrid, himself, beside this monster success of mediocrity, would be looked upon as mild: *'beau bien sûre, mais pas dans le mouvement,'*" If to the *Propositions, The Red Rag* is added, that lucid explanation of *Arrangements* and *Harmonies* as titles for his pictures, you have the very bones and sinews of his technical practice and teaching. In the Académie Carmen a copy of *Propositions— No. 2* hung upon the walls.

On the whole, to the serious rather than to the joyous Whistler *The Gentle Art* is the monument. The letters might be left out and, though a pity to lose them, *The Action, Ten O'Clock, Art and Art Critics*, the *Propositions, The Red Rag* would more than make up for their loss. To the world and to art Whistler the Artist is of more importance than Whistler the Man. For this reason I would also include with the writing to be preserved at all hazards at least one letter—his amazing letter to Swinburne, replete with not only his seriousness but his sensitiveness, his tenderness, his sorrow for the blow dealt by a fellow artist—an artist in words. The critic he could throw into the gutter

"rather cursorily," as he threw Tom Taylor. But
to be foully misrepresented by a poet— and he the
poet who had translated into his medium the strange
loveliness of *The Little White Girl*—was too cruel
a wound for Whistler to pretend to make light
of it. In *The Fortnightly Review* (June, 1888)
Swinburne wrote an article on *Ten O'Clock*. All
the foolish jibes of the critics reappeared in it,
all the old foolish names were called—jester, tum-
bler, clown, dotard, dunce, with, here and there,
a compliment, a condescending recognition grudgingly granted. But the tendency of the article to
ridicule, to expose the "gospel of the grin," there
was no mistaking, and Whistler was hurt to the
quick:

"Why, O brother!" he wrote, "did you not con-
sult with me before printing, in the face of a
ribald world, *that you also misunderstood,* and are
capable of saying so, with vehemence and repetition.

.   .   .   .

"Cannot the man who wrote *Atalanta*—and the
Ballads beautiful—can he not be content to spend
his life with *his* work, which should be his love,—
and has for him no misleading doubt and darkness
—that he should so stray about blindly in his
brother's flower-beds and bruise himself!

.   .   .   .

"Who are you, deserting your Muse, that you

should insult my Goddess with familiarity, and the manners of approach common to the reasoners in the market place. . . .

"Do we not speak the same language? Are we strangers, then, or, in our Father's house, are there so many mansions that you lose your way, my brother, and cannot recognize your kin?

.   .   .   .

"You have been misled—you have mistaken the pale demeanor and joined hands for an outward and visible sign of an inward and spiritual earnestness. For you, these are the serious ones, and, for them, you others are the serious matter! Their joke is their work. For me—why should I refuse myself the grim joy of this grotesque tragedy—and, with them now, you all are my joke!"

To be sure, he gave Swinburne in *The World* a sharp Butterfly sting that probably tingled and smarted. The title is *Freeing a Last Friend,* and it winds up, "Thank you, my dear! I have lost a *confrère,* but then, I have gained an acquaintance —one Algernon Swinburne—'outsider'—Putney." For Swinburne was by this time under the grandmotherly charge of Watts-Dunton, living a sober life at The Pines in suburban Putney. Of the two, this letter has doubtless been the oftener read. But the first—*Et tu, Brute!*—is a genuine cry from the real Whistler, from the artist up in arms when the dignity of art was attacked.

FANNY LEYLAND

Whistler, before the end of the Nineties, published another book, his report of the Eden Trial:
The Baronet and the Butterfly. It has the interest
of everything that concerns Whistler, though not
the brilliancy and wit of *The Gentle Art*. The reason for this Trial perhaps is not forgotten. But the
world forgets quickly and I had better state it in
a few words, as a reminder. Whistler had painted
Lady Eden's portrait, arranging through George
Moore that the price was to be from one hundred
to one hundred and fifty pounds for a sketch in
pastel or water-color. Lady Eden was beautiful, a
sitter to his taste, and he painted a small half-
length in oils. When it was finished Sir William
Eden chose the fourteenth of February as date of
payment and, in the studio, presented Whistler
with a "Valentine" in an envelope. When Whistler
opened the envelope he found a check for the lowest sum mentioned, one hundred, and it was in
pounds, not in guineas. He thought, rightly, that
it was for him to decide upon the price and he
could no more forgive Sir William Eden for the
pounds instead of guineas than Leyland in the old
quarrel over the Peacock Room. He kept—to make
sure of bringing things to a crisis, he deposited—
the check, he refused to give up the painting. Sir
William sued him in the French Courts, for this
happened when Whistler was living in Paris. In
the Civil Tribunal Whistler lost. He took the case

to the *Cour de Cassation* and won. He was allowed
to keep the painting which, for him, was all that
counted. He had to pay back the hundred pounds
as he had meant to. Also, he had to pay the costs
of the first Trial, but Sir William Eden had to pay
the costs of the Appeal. Out of these proceedings
Whistler made his book. Except for the comments
on the margin and the prodigious antics of the
Butterfly, there is little Whistler in it, and lawyers'
pleadings are not often amusing reading. I thought
his reports to us in his letters not only more read-
able but more illuminating. In these he explained
that he had proved the right of an artist to his own
work, added a new clause to the *Code Napoléon*
and, incidentally "wiped up the floor" with the
Baronet, while all Paris looked on. And the news
of it must be spread.

"Take my word for it," was the way he put it
to Joseph Pennell, "the first duty of a good general
when he has won his battle is to say so, otherwise
the people, always dull—the Briton especially—
fail to understand, and it is an unsettled point in
history forever. Victory is not complete until the
wounded are looked after and the dead counted."

To his private correspondence he gave no less
care than to his books and his letters for the public.
The hope is that some day this correspondence may
be published. The letter might be to a friend or on
business, but he could not let it go with a slovenly

sentence or a slovenly page. I have a vivid memory
of the day he asked me to dictate to him a letter
he had written to his shoemaker in Paris, because,
having made corrections in the original, he wished
to have a fair copy to send. And my memory is as
vivid of his pains in addressing the envelope to
"M.——, *Maître Bottier*." His letters were as beautiful to look at as they were stimulating to read.
They were designed as well as written. I emphasize
the point because, until they are published, the new
generation cannot quite realize how essentially he
was the artist in little things as in great, his sense
of beauty so keen that he could never be satisfied
with anything short of perfection. Unless this fact
is recognized Whistler must remain an enigma to
the ordinary man. I have heard contemptuous
words poured upon him, by an artist who should
have known better, because, before going into a
dinner or a reception, he would look in the glass,
give a touch to his hair, to his ribbon of a necktie—
another scandal—to the set of his coat. I often saw
him do this in our place before going into the room
where he was to preside at an International meeting. But I watched him with admiration, knowing
it was not vanity on his part but that unquench-
able striving after perfection, in himself as in his
art, in everything that belonged to him.

VII

WHISTLER THE ARTIST: HIS WIT

FOR long in London Whistler's fame was greater as a wit than as an artist, not that people understood his wit better than his art but they imagined they did. When a man says something witty the point may be missed, as it often was in Whistler's case, but laughter is appropriate according to the rules of the game. When Whistler painted a picture those who laughed loudest could not have been so sure that laughter was the correct tribute.

The wonder is that his wit was accepted even on trust, so fundamentally unlike was it to the kind familiar to his public. It was keen, light, sharp, swift. Critics fell upon him with bludgeons of stupidity and he parried their blows with graceful rapier-like thrusts to which they were unaccustomed. But if his weapon was delicate, it could be cruel and he would not have had it otherwise. It could wound and he was far from unwilling that it should. Not until "the enemies" were cruel beyond endurance did he begin to use his wit in self-defense. The witticisms so often repeated, of

FIRELIGHT, JOSEPH PENNELL, NO. I

such inexhaustible help to the journalist with an
odd corner of his newspaper to fill, belong to the
years when it had become the fashion to look
down upon him as a jester and upon his art as a
jest. He was never cruel during the gay years in
Paris, never cruel during those early years in London before his gayety had been embittered. His
fun at first bubbled up without a shadow to its
joyousness. In those days he had no desire to wound.
He preferred to laugh *with* rather than *at* people.
I have already recalled his comment when Rossetti
showed him the picture and read him the sonnet
inspired by the same subject: "Why not frame the
sonnet?" But this was no doubt not intended
to be unkind. His affection for Rossetti was genuine. More probably it was too spontaneous a criticism to be suppressed, spontaneity being the very
essence of his wit, though the last quality it was
given credit for.

Most people think that if an artist can paint
or draw or carve, other accomplishments are superfluous. Book learning and political opinions are
not supposed to come his way; wit and humor are
unwarranted distractions from his appointed task
in life. It was the habit of Whistler's contemporaries to treat art with portentous solemnity. Because he had other accomplishments, they refused
to see good or greatness in his paintings. As they
could not deny his wit, they tried to explain it

away by saying he prepared his witticisms laboriously and led up to them ingeniously when in any company he was determined to impress, electrify, or insult. Nothing could be more unlike Whistler. His wit was part of his joy in living, his contribution to the gayety of nations; he would have disdained it had he been compelled to force it out with hammer and tongs. Harper Pennington, when he wrote out his impressions for Joseph Pennell and myself, said that only once did he see Whistler "stumped for a reply." It was no wonder he was then, for Lady Meux, posing in her sables, told him to "keep a civil tongue in that head of yours or I will have in some one to *finish* those portraits you have made of me." What ready answer could have been forthcoming to that sort of Billingsgate? We never "saw" him "stumped" once, while we did see him on the most difficult occasion possible readier with his answer than was exactly appreciated by his opponent.

He had come as a witness on our side in the lawsuit which Joseph Pennell brought against *The Saturday Review*. It had published an article on Lithography in which a reviewer suggested that lithographs as Joseph Pennell made them on transfer paper were not lithographs, and that to ask the same price for them as for lithographs made on stone was to mislead the public as to their commercial value. The lithographer does not have to

be told what nonsense this is, but a public, without
a shred of technical understanding, will believe
most things it reads about art in a paper supposed to be authoritative. The statement affected
Whistler as seriously for, with a few exceptions, his
lithographs were all done on transfer paper. In the
course of cross-examination reference was made
to Mr. Walter Sickert, who wrote the article, and
Whistler described him as "an insignificant and
irresponsible person."

"Then," said the Counsel for the other side, "Mr.
Sickert is an insignificant and irresponsible person
who can do no harm."

To which, in a flash, Whistler: "Even a fool can
do harm."

Again, later on in the cross-examination, when
it was hinted that he was helping to pay our costs
and our Counsel, to put this straight, asked him if
there was "any foundation for the question?"

"Only the lightness and delicacy of the Counsel's
suggestion," said Whistler.

Those answers show his swiftness in finding the
right, the cutting, the witty answer in the witness
box, the hardest of hard places to be swift and
witty in. Whatever Whistler's wit lacked, it was
never spontaneity.

I recall lighter occasions when his readiness
served him as well. I was dining with Heinemann,
the publisher. There was much talk of the French,

much depreciation with which Whistler was wholly
out of sympathy. At last, some one objected to the
manners of the French because they were all on
the surface. "Well, you know, a very good place
to have them!" was Whistler's comment. Another
evening, during the Boer War, which furnished him
with innumerable opportunities at the expense of
the British, some one told him the latest news was
that Buller had "retired" without losing a man, or
a flag, or a cannon, "Yes, or a minute," Whistler
added. I remember his answer when I asked how
he liked that wonderful portrait Boldini painted of
him, "Well, they say that looks like me but I hope
I don't look like that," and his telling somebody at
our dinner table of his sitters who gradually began
to look like his portraits of them. For the answer,
the comment, the criticism, there was no waiting.
He was always ready, never required time to think
it out, to prepare it.

His encounters with Oscar Wilde have passed
into history. He and Wilde were the two most
conspicuous figures in the social London of the
Eighties. They were often compared as wits but
there was no comparison. Oscar was witty but his
wit seems more labored, more carefully worked
out and he could borrow and adapt from others
when at a loss. That is the explanation of the often-
told story: Oscar's "I wish I had said that, Whistler," and Whistler's "You will, Oscar, you will."

NOCTURNE (*Lithotint*)

Whistler, in the beginning, was friendly with
Wilde, thought him clever, fancied he really knew
something about art. Wilde was clever, but of art
his knowledge was, as the lady thought the manners of the French—on the surface. He had grown
up under influences Whistler least respected. He
had taken part in that extraordinary Oxford movement, had made roads under Ruskin, who encouraged road-making somehow for the good of art; he
had steeped himself in the traditions of Pre-Rapha-
elitism, had come in at the tail end of the craze for
Blue China and fancied himself apostle of all it
symbolized. An author and a wit, it has been said,
should have a separate costume, a particular cloth
—Whistler did not quite believe this, he dressed at
first to please himself and afterwards, discovering
the shock it gave, to annoy a conventional public.
Wilde flaunted his knee breeches and velvet jacket
and long hair as a sign of esthetic salvation. This was
the reason for Whistler's *Just Indignation* in *The
Gentle Art*. Oscar had invented new sacramental
garments and displayed himself in a Polish cap
and a much befrogged, much befurred green overcoat:

"Oscar—How dare you! What means this dis-
guise!

"Restore those things to Nathan's and never
again let me find you masquerading the streets of

my Chelsea in the combined costumes of Kossuth and Mr. Mantalini!"

To Whistler, Wilde's pose was affectation, and affectation in connection with art, Whistler could not stand. The friendship did not last. When it came to an end Whistler was merciless. He never lost an opportunity to challenge Oscar, and their duel of wit was one of the most amusing incidents in Edmund Yates' *World*. Their letters scattered the "choice venom" of this wit through its pages and were never unwelcome to Atlas who, it must be said for him, was a confirmed enemy to dullness.

Oscar, in Exeter at the time, wired to Whistler after reading a skit in *Punch*: "*Punch* too ridiculous—when you and I are together we never talk about anything except ourselves."

Whistler wired back: "No, no, Oscar, you forget—when you and I are together, we never talk about anything except me."

And Atlas rejoiced in recording the clash of arms.

Oscar sometimes showed Whistler that truest form of flattery by appropriating his opinions and statements. But when, to save his respect, he backed himself by the earlier plagiarist who said "I take my good there where I find it," "Excellent," Whistler thought, but Oscar could go further and boast, "I take *his* good there where I find it."

A poisoned arrow this that went home and Oscar

in his answer was amazingly dignified, holding
Whistler up to scorn as "an ill-bred and ignorant
person." The Butterfly fairly danced over his dis-
play of temper, its tail curling up with wicked
rapture. "I am awe-stricken and tremble," Whistler wrote, "for truly the rage of the sheep is
terrible." And he gave another telling thrust when
Oscar, talking at the Club of the Academy Students, had gone forth, Whistler wrote, "on that
occasion as my St. John—but, forgetting that
humility should be his chief characteristic and un-
able to withstand the unaccustomed respect with
which his utterances were received, he not only
trifled with my shoe, but bolted with the latchet!"

It was not all fun on Whistler's part; there was,
as always, the laugh for the world. But he never
forgave and Oscar, roused, could be insulting.
Neither could Whistler forget. I remember years
afterwards when Oscar was in Reading Gaol and
the few among his old friends still with the courage to call themselves friends, started a petition
to shorten the length of his term, Robert Ross—
that friend of friends—asked me to intercede with
Whistler and beg him to sign the petition—his
name would carry such weight. Whistler refused.
He would not pass himself off as the friend he was
not, nor pretend compassion for the man who
fared only as he deserved.

Some pages in *The Gentle Art* may have lost

their savor. The people they concern, if insignificant in their time, are in ours forgotten and not worth resurrecting. Or the events that caused the correspondence have long ceased to be of consequence. All the same, the book as a whole is a complete revelation of Whistler the artist, serious and sincere, a characteristic chronicle of Whistler the man, witty, whimsical, "wicked." The Butterfly, bowing in mock deference to *"Messieurs les Ennemis"* on the opening page gives the keynote to this "wickedness." After reading the various episodes you cannot wonder at the fear in which he was held. He was unfailing in his detection of the enemy's weak point, unerring in his aim of the little barbed arrows. Take the page where he quotes Hamerton's confession of laughter, with the crowd, in front of *The White Girl* when it hung in the *Salon* of the Refused. Whistler adds nothing of his own but on the margin, side by side with the confession, simply prints Hamerton's opinion of Corot's paintings as the sketches of an amateur, his assertion that whatever Courbet touched he made unpleasant, his scorn of Daubigny who is without either drawing or color; and then his praise of Gustave Doré as "the most imaginative, the profoundest, the most productive poet that has ever sprung from the French race"—this finished Hamerton as a critic. In that catalogue of his etchings in which Whistler quotes, after each

THE SMITH PASSAGE DU DRAGON

entry, a former criticism of his unfortunate critics, he has another dig at Hamerton who had previously found "so little" in the prints; on the margin is Hamerton's dictum that "the Thames is beautiful from Maidenhead to Kent, but not from Battersea to Sheerness" which were the reaches Whistler made immortal in his Thames etchings. Wedmore is quoted: "He—Whistler—took from London to Venice his happy fashion of suggesting lapping water." Whistler's "Reflection" on the margin: "Like Eno's fruit salt or the *Anti-mal-de-mer!*" And so Whistler kept it up all through, to the end of the catalogue and the last words on the last page: "We roar all like bears," the Butterfly kicking joyously.

There was wit of another kind when he wrote that the visit planned to his own country, established as an impossibility, had of course become true, "for one cannot continually disappoint a Continent!" Or his description of Mortimer Menpes, who had been adapting one of his schemes of decoration: "an Australian immigrant who, like the kangaroo of his country, is born with a pocket and puts everything into it," followed by the wired advice: "You will blow your brains out, of course. Pigott has shown you what to do under the circumstances, and you know your way to Spain. Good-by!" It is scarcely necessary to add that this was at the time of the scandal of the Parnell letters in *The Times*. He was collecting scalps, he used to say to account for these little barbed arrows. "And yet, O Atlas," he explained in *The World,* "they say that I cannot keep a friend—my dear, I cannot afford it—and *you* only keep for me their scalps." His advice to the lady who complained of the trouble her friends gave her was: "Do as I do, Madame, lose them."

To go on quoting would be but to make *The Gentle Art* over again. His talk was as full of the same delightful touches. He never could say anything like anybody else. I recall his description of Rome, where he went for the first time in 1899 to be "best man" at Heinemann's wedding at Porto d'Anzio close by: "a bit of an old ruin alongside of a railway station, where I saw Mrs. Potter Palmer!" And his remark when Henley criticized his design of a gallows for the cover of one of Heinemann's books as too slight, in need of a support. "Well, you know, that's the usual sort of gallows, but this one will do. It will hang all of us. Just like Henley's selfishness to want a strong one." At a dinner, when religion was the subject, and some one asked him "And what are you, Mr. Whistler?" "I, madam? Why, I am an amateur." And his retort to the Englishman who thought "the trouble is, we English are too honest, we have always been stupidly honest." "You see," said Whistler, "whenever there has been honesty in this country, there has been stupidity." The Briton, from whom he had suffered much, remained always a fruitful subject of jest. The popular Bath Club in London he called "the latest incarnation of the British discovery of water." Back from a journey on a P. and O. boat, he described how at dinner all the men and all the stewards were in dinner jackets, all the women in low gowns, no matter how sea-sick, "Well, you know," he said to me, "you might as well dress to ride in an omnibus." In a speech at a dinner in Paris, he pointed out the difference of method in English and French Art Schools: "Now, as to teaching, in England it is all a matter of taste, but in France at least they tell you which end of the brush to stick in your mouth." Naturally, Whistler was not always welcome at an English dinner party. He said to me once: "Well, you know, when I'm asked out to dinner, I always enjoy myself. But—well—I'm never asked to the same house twice."

He could frighten away the most ardent collector of his work. An American, who had managed to force himself into the Studio, asked him:

"How much for the whole lot, Mr. Whistler?"

"Five millions."

"What?"

"My posthumous prices."

But the stories are endless. A favorite, often published, is of Whistler buying a hat in a hat store, an irate customer rushing in and mistaking him for a salesman, shouting to him, "I say this hat doesn't fit," and Whistler, looking him up and down: "Your coat don't either." Another, often repeated, is of the sitter who was not satisfied with his portrait, "Do you call it a good piece of art?" he asked. "Well, do you call yourself a good piece of Nature?" asked Whistler.

In one respect Whistler's wit must seem out of fashion to the new generation, for he was ever reticent on subjects nowadays considered essentially "good form" in the schoolroom as in the parlor. It has been recorded of his talk that it was exceptionally "clean." He had no use for what were of old "smoking-room stories." This was my experience and it was Joseph Pennell's as well. Once only did I know him to venture on what to him was unsavory ground. We were talking of a country house scandal going the rounds in London. "Well, you know," was Whistler's conclusion, "for weekends the rule should be to ring a loud bell at five in the morning, after which guests are expected to be found in no rooms save their own." From Whistler this was extreme, mild as it must seem to our young people brought up on to-day's best sellers and raided dramas. I would not give the impression that there was the slightest touch of the prude about him. He was too wise, too what Henley would have called "human." Prudishness in-

ST. ANNE'S, SOHO

ensed him. Horsley, an Academic Comstock, at
a Church Congress during Whistler's British Artists' episode, had been talking rubbish about the
"degradations" of the model's "shameful calling"
and so on. Whistler sent a nude to the next British
Artists' Exhibition. Underneath it he wrote:
"*Horsley soit qui mal y pense,*" and Horsley never
outlived it.

It is difficult to give a just idea of Whistler's
wit because his manner, his personality was such
a part of it. His own enjoyment was so keen it became contagious. He was sometimes surprised himself that his inspiration should be so sudden and
so sure. "Providence," he would say, "is kind and
sends me these little things." And he was by no
means the last to appreciate his good things.
Drouet, the sculptor and old student friend, told
us of a winter evening in Paris towards the end
when Whistler, old and ill, tired and fearfully de-
pressed, was going out to dinner much against his
inclination. It was in the days of the old-fashioned
horse cab when the same fare was paid for every
ride, whatever the distance, and Whistler was going far. It was bitter cold and he took a cab with
the *chauffrette* sign. Presently he found there was
no *chauffrette* inside and he saw it outside under
the *cocher's* feet. He got to the end of his drive,
frozen, miserable, ill-tempered. He paid the exact
fare. The *cocher* raged: "And where is the *pour-*

boire?" "Inside, on the *chauffrette*," said Whistler, and no cocktail could have been a better stimulant. He forgot his misery, and his friends at the dinner had not known him so gay for years.

A deaf man, watching him, could not have helped enjoying his stories and his witticisms. His whole face lit up, his deep-set eyes under their heavy eyebrows glittered and flamed and laughed, his hands seemed to talk, his eloquent hands, slim, long, flexible. Boldini, in his portrait, caught their character. "His exquisite hands, never at rest," Arthur Symons describes them. As I write, I am more and more conscious of the impossibility of giving Whistler's wit its full value unless an adequate impression of his personality can be conveyed with it. In memory, I cannot separate his personality from the thing said. I see him always in our Buckingham Street dining-room, where such long hours were spent, such long discussions held, so many stories told over our dinner table, he always in his special place, which was in front of the fire because he never could be warm enough. I see his deep blue eyes flaring and dancing under the unforgettable eyebrows, his hands, in their rapid, ceaseless movement, punctuating, underlining, emphasizing his every word, his lips drawn up with that "wicked," quizzical expression which was half laugh, half joy in one of the little things Providence never failed to send him; the mobile, expressive mouth which Boldini also caught in his sympathetic portrait. If there were occasions when Whistler "felt like a little devil,"—"Really, I do believe I am a devil like Barnaby Rudge's raven"—Boldini's portrait comes nearer showing him in that mood, arrayed in his armor against *Messieurs les Ennemis,* than any other I know. So long as Whistler's talk and writings survive in published records, his reputation for wit cannot be denied him. But the charm and the gayety he brought to that wit have gone with the man. Those who knew him are fast dwindling in numbers and the world, presently, must believe in the power of his personality as best it can from the testimony bequeathed to it by the few who loved and the many who feared him.

VIII

WHISTLER THE MAN AND THE ARTIST: HIS TRIUMPH

WHISTLER won the battle, the tide turned in his favor, while he had still a few years in which to enjoy the victory.

Several things had happened to bring this about. His Presidency of the British Artists, though it ended in the usual public howls of foolish laughter, was not without its effect. It implied official recognition. The fact that some members of the Society resigned with him was more important, for it was a public acknowledgment that artists were not all against him. Younger men were breaking loose from the conventions of the old school and they hailed him as the Master and proclaimed themselves the "Followers." The new generation meant a new opposition, a new secession. Oppositions, like other matters, are apt to be ordered with less outward enthusiasm in England than elsewhere, but by the beginning of the Nineties the power of the old Academic set was waning though the signs were as yet scarcely visible. The keener of vision detected one sign in the New

THE CONVALESCENT

English Art Club, founded in the Eighties and attracting most of the younger men of promise. To see now the work they were exhibiting then is to marvel at the restraint of their revolution. At the time, however, according to Academic standards, it was anything but restrained; to the average man who, in those days, figured as "the man in the street," it was somewhat incomprehensible, to artists a fine assertion of independence. I recall a Private View, where I met Félix Buhot, and the gleam in his rather wild eyes as we made the rounds together. "I smell the powder," he said. Buhot was always extravagant, fantastic in his personality as in the strange little afterthoughts overflowing on the margin of his prints. There was powder, but only for the most sensitive nostrils. What Whistler had to do with it all was evident on every side, for in the work of this young group he was the prevailing influence, the master to be studied, whose tradition was to be carried on.

Another factor in his favor was the appearance of a new group of critics, the development of a new school of criticism. The Hamertons and the Wedmores no longer had it entirely their own way, no longer were alone in possession. Any one with as keen a scent as Buhot began to smell the powder in the critical columns of the more enterprising papers. Towards the end of the Eighties *The Star* was founded in London, a half-penny afternoon

paper appealing especially to "the people," and yet
with a more brilliant staff than many of the old
well-established sheets could boast. A. B. Walkley
wrote the dramatic column, Le Gallienne the literary column, George Bernard Shaw the art column
which he promptly relinquished for the music
column and, at his suggestion, art was handed
over to the care of Joseph Pennell. I had not yet
met Whistler, Joseph Pennell knew him only
slightly, but he did know Whistler's work well
and, young as he was, had recognized its greatness
and distinction before he left America. What
Joseph Pennell thought with conviction, he had a
way all his life of saying and writing with em-
phasis, a fact which his present reputation has
established beyond a doubt. Whistler triumphed
as master in *The Star* as on the walls of the New
English Art Club, R.O.M.—"Bob"—Stevenson was
The Pall Mall's art critic, and training in Paris and
Barbizon had long since freed him from Academic
prejudice. There was also D. S. MacColl, just up
from Oxford, writing for *The Spectator*, and there
was Charles Whibley, Henley's art "young man"
on *The Scots Observer*. Here were four writers
with a talent for forcible writing and young enough
not to have lost their enthusiasm. Thus, at last,
Whistler had "Followers" and critics to uphold
him.

He had waited long for success, but when it

came it was without stint. In 1891 the Glasgow Corporation bought his *Carlyle* painted almost twenty years before. The bargain was not without haggling. Whistler's price was one thousand guineas. The deputation from Glasgow, being Scotch, protested against such a price and asked him to think it over. The next day, returning to his studio, they said: "Well, Mr. Whistler, have you thought it over?" And Whistler said, "Why, gentlemen,—well, you know, how could I think of anything but the pleasure of seeing you again?" And, telling the story, he added: "And, naturally, being gentlemen, they understood, and they gave me a check for the thousand guineas."

The same year, 1891, the *Mother* was bought for the Luxembourg. There was no haggling over the price. The payment, when the French Government invests in works of art, is in the honor done to the artist, and the Luxembourg, meaning everything to Whistler as the first step to the Louvre, he was content with the nominal sum of four thousand francs. His chief satisfaction was in the choice of the *Mother* for "so solemn a consecration." It should not be forgotten that the picture was bought on the initiative of M. Clemenceau. When exhibited in Philadelphia and New York, in 1881-82, it could have been bought for one thousand dollars, and not a gallery, not a collector would face so risky an investment. The whirligig of time has not been slow in bringing about its revenge, and the portrait to-day hangs in the Louvre where it was Whistler's dearest ambition to see it.

Mr. David Croal Thomson, then managing the Goupil Gallery in London, was the first to realize practically how complete had been the change in the attitude towards Whistler, the first with the courage to seize the critical moment in the turning of the tide and to propose a retrospective exhibition. He would have restricted it to the portraits. But Whistler was always wise, though few might credit him with wisdom. He decided for all his paintings. By their variety would he challenge "the enemies" for years warring against him, bent upon his destruction. No half-measures were to weaken his "heroic kick in Bond Street," as he called the Exhibition. He was right. The variety stupefied the old critics who had never believed, it took away the breath of the young critics who overflowed with faith but who had never seen the earlier pictures. Every stage in his development was represented. Here were the paintings done under Courbet's influence, the Japanese pictures, the noble succession of full-length portraits and the Nocturnes. The Press View is fresh in my memory, for I was there as, by this time, I was writing art criticism, beginning to play understudy to Joseph Pennell in his London papers and taking

Stillman's place on the New York *Nation*. The
excitement was tense, the younger group exulting
in this justification of their faith, the older group
a trifle subdued and bewildered anew. The success
of the Exhibition with the Press was overwhelming
and Whistler was receiving reports of his triumph
in one of the inner sanctuaries of the Gallery.

The result was inevitable. Day after day the
Gallery was crowded. Whistlers began to change
hands and to sell for large sums. People did not
have to be asked to sit for their portraits. They
clamored for the privilege. Rich Americans be-
sieged him, eager "to pour California into his lap."
He did not object, his pockets, he thought, should
always be full if his golden eggs were not to be
addled. An amazing future opened out before him,
a future of ease in which he could do the work that
waited to be done, free from the old anxiety and
continual strain. His worst enemy could not
grudge him this one unclouded interval, it was so
miserably short. The first shadow, light perhaps
but deeply resented, was the traffic in his pictures,
not by strangers but by friends and relations to
whom he had presented them or sold them for a
song during his numerous financial crises. Where
he had received pounds, they were getting their
thousands. It was what always happens under the
circumstances but that did not make it easier to
bear, and he raged against the "so-called friends"

who were "turning his reputation into pounds, shillings and pence, traveling over Europe and holiday-making on the profits."

The other shadow was heavier and its darkness never altogether lifted. The Goupil Exhibition had exalted him to a pedestal high enough to satisfy the most ambitious. He was living again in the Paris he loved, with a beautiful apartment on the Rue du Bac and a big studio on the Rue Notre-Dame-des-Champs. His countrymen were giving up their long policy of distrust and neglect and flocking to his studio. He was asked to join with Puvis de Chavannes, Sargent and Abbey in decorating the Boston Library. Years of fine work and the comfort of prosperity seemed ahead of him when the crushing blow fell, the one blow in his life against which he could not react. He had married in 1888 the widow of W. E. Godwin, architect of the White House. "'The fascinating Widdie' and I are now the Whistlers," he wrote to Waldo Story at the time, "people who really were meant for each other from the beginning." And the heroic kick in Bond Street had scarcely cleared the way for further triumphs when his wife fell ill. Month by month, week by week, day by day, it was his fate to watch her fading away in the agony of cancer before, in 1896, death came to release her and to leave him again alone, broken in health and spirit.

THE BEACH

This was the period when I saw him often and
intimately. In sorrow, as in happiness, he could
not bear to stay by himself. But there was a difference. In sorrow the only people whose company
he could endure were friends upon whose sympathy and understanding he could count. When
he was in London and we were at home, he would
come to us to dine sometimes three or four evenings a week. For months he would share William
Heinemann's flat. Not that he was without places
of his own. For a time he had his apartment, his
studio and a room in the Hotel Chatham in Paris
and in London a studio and a room in Garlant's
Hotel—no wonder he would jest over his "collection of *châteaux* and *pieds-à-terre*," though the expense frightened him. He was not used to having
money. Once, during those last years, he asked
Heinemann to go to his Bank and find out if anything was left in his account, and Heinemann
found a nice little balance of over six thousand
pounds. Heinemann's friendship was a stimulus
and a support and his flat in Whitehall Court was
conveniently close to Buckingham Street. In the
intimacy that from now on strengthened, we became more conscious than ever of the two sides
to Whistler that seemed a contradiction and made
him incomprehensible to the crowd. No evenings
in my life have been gayer than those he spent
with us. He might arrive sad and weary but,

gradually, with the rest and the good talk and th
good dinner—for he approved of the dinners ou
French Augustine cooked for him—he relaxed
forgot for the time. He lived over the past, tol
us the old stories, recalled the old duels with "th
enemies"—told and recalled them as no one els
could or can. This does not mean that he was in
different to the present. He kept up with th
times, was aware of everything going on, whethe
the last defeat in South Africa or the last scanda
in the studios. He loved gossip, would be quit
indignant if I had gathered none in my rounds o
the galleries or the course of my visits. He was sur
I had a cupboard full of skeletons and, careful a
I was, one day they would all come rattling dow
about my ears.

He was as rigid in his opinions as ever, woul
not yield an inch if art as the "science of beauty"
was questioned or his theories disputed. Over th
dinner table he and Joseph Pennell would figh
evening after evening until I would say to myself
this surely is the end. One excited evening, with
the bang of Whistler's knife on the table a pictur
tumbled down from the wall, the glass shattered
in a hundred pieces. I waited, trembling. But Whis
tler was enchanted—even the pictures argued fo.
him. The popular idea was that he could not stand
contradiction, "I am not arguing with you—I an
telling you," was one of his favorite sayings and

t was taken to mean that not to agree with him
was the end of his friendship. But our experience
was that talk without contradiction would have
eemed as flat to him as dinner without wine.
Joseph Pennell was no more a man of peace than
Whistler, nothing could keep him from speaking
he truth that was in him. They often disagreed,
but were only the friendlier, only appreciated each
other the more for their tournament of talk. It was
he toady who offended beyond forgiveness.

As time went on Whistler was glad enough to
meet people—congenial people—in our place, and
all who met him there succumbed to the spell of
his gayety and charm. From this gayety the bitterness had all but vanished, for "the enemies" had all
but disappeared. Only once was I present when the
old anger flared up and the old enemy withered
before it. Joseph Pennell was lecturing on Lithography at the Society of Arts, and Whistler went to
the lecture with me. At the end, as we got up to
go and were starting to leave the lecture hall, a
hand was stretched out from the row behind us
and a voice said, "Come now, Mr. Whistler, be a
gentleman and shake hands with me." Whistler
drew himself up, the danger signals in his eyes:
"It is because I am a gentleman that I refuse to
shake hands with you," and he walked on, I trembling at his heels. Something of the same kind happened one afternoon when Joseph Pennell was

walking with him somewhere near Charing-Cross.
They met a well-known architect who ran to him
with hand outstretched, "Why, Jimmie, I have
not seen you for years." Whistler put up his
monocle and stared at the architect. "Joseph," he
said, "who is this person?" Those who had turned
their backs upon him or who, he thought, had
wronged him, in the years of persecution, he would
not take into his arms because they changed their
tactics with his changing fortunes.

Whistler's gayety never let me lose sight of his
seriousness. Art was the supreme interest. People,
gossip, argument could not hold him when art
beckoned. Sometimes I feared that his absorption
in it during the day would hasten the end. He was
in a fever of work, full of schemes and commis-
sions. There was so much still to be done, so little
time to do it in, he often said, he was just beginning to learn and, with knowledge, what could he
not accomplish. He was painting the series of portraits of children, he was busy with his last large
full-lengths, some of which were never finished,
some worked over to their ruin. He was doing his
little pastels of draped figures. His water-color box
went with him in his wanderings through the
streets. The little case of transfer paper was almost
always in his pocket. During the summer, on the
northern coast of France, or near Dublin, or among
the dunes of Holland, he was painting, sketching,

working incessantly. He never stopped except for
the days he spent, reluctantly, in bed, except for
the evening after the light had faded, though even
then it was not easy to drag him from his easel.
To the end, if the two clashed, the seriousness of
the artist overpowered the gayety of the man.

The days in bed grew more frequent. Sorrow
had left its mark. Hard work began to tell. The
very last years were sadness itself. A subdued Whistler with only occasional flashes of the old gayety,
a Whistler preoccupied with his health, a Whistler
breaking his heart over the loss of time—this was
not a Whistler his friends found pleasure in seeing.
Sometimes I was tempted to wish that the end had
come during the summer of 1902 when he was
desperately ill in The Hague. His life was despaired
of. But he recovered and, with his recovery, the
old wit seemed to revive. Bulletins of his condition,
some most alarming, had been sent daily to the
London papers and when, at last, news followed of
his convalescence, *The Morning Post* published an
article that obviously had been prepared for an
obituary. With something of the old joy that filled
the letters to Atlas, he wrote to *The Morning Post*
to beg that the "ready wreath and quick biography
might be put back into their pigeonhole for later
use" and, reference having been made to his still
luxuriantly thick hair, he added an apology for
"continuing to wear my own hair and eyebrows

after distinguished *confrères* and eminent person
have long ceased the habit."

A melancholy Whistler he was when he got back
to London, the ghost of the Whistler who ha
laughed his troubles away and scattered his enemie
with the first dart of the Butterfly's sting. A
Whistler with shrunken face and with eyes that
through the long last winter, were ready to shu
in sleep after a few minutes' talk—a Whistler dis
daining a dressing gown, symbol of illness, an
tottering about the studio in the familiar lon;
brown overcoat reaching to his heels—anythin;
but the "dandy" Whistler he had always rejoiced
in being since the West Point days when he liked
to remember himself as "very dandy in gray."
Now and then in London, as in The Hague, h
rallied. When Canfield, the gambler, whose por
trait he was painting, bought the *Rosa Corde*
from Graham Robertson, it was in his studio again
and a wire bade us come "to make your *adieux* to
her before her departure for America," and I begar
to hope as I stood by him while he wiped the can
vas here and there with a soft silk handkerchie:
and asked me if she was not beautiful. It was on
of the rare good days. He was triumphant when
another day, he showed his *Daughter of Eve,* won
derful then but spoiled by him later, to Joseph
Pennell and said he had painted it that very morn
ing in a couple of hours. A few letters were writte:

o the papers. He kept in touch with the affairs
f the International Society. He contributed to
n exhibition of old silver at the Fine Art Society's.
Ie had surprising moments, but they were only
noments. One knew all the time the end was in-
vitable and there was no surprise when it came
uddenly on Friday, July 17, 1903.

The funeral service was at old Chelsea Church
n Cheyne Walk, to which on many Sunday morn-
ngs he had walked with his mother, leaving her
t the door. He was buried in old Chiswick Grave-
ard at his wife's side. Westminster or St. Paul's
rypt would seem a more fitting place for the
nost distinguished artist who worked in England
luring the Nineteenth Century. But at Chiswick
Vhistler lies not far from Hogarth, whose art he
oved as a boy in St. Petersburg, and up to whom
e looked with reverence all his life as England's
;reatest master. And so, these two great men sleep
n this remote suburban graveyard, as William
'enn sleeps in lonely Jordan's, and the simplicity
f their last home is as it should be, for their monu-
nent is in their art, and as artists they will live
orever.

The publishers wish to express their appreciation to Mr. Elmer Adler, The Boston Museum, The Carnegie Institute, The Freer Collection, Frederick Keppel & Co., The Kraushaar Galleries, The Metropolitan Museum, The National Gallery in London and the New York Public Library, for their cooperation in making the publication of this volume possible.